VINDICATION!

The New Woman.

HAVE DINNER READY AT ONE O'CLOCK, JOHN!

Ian McDonald
VINDICATION!

A Postcard History of the Women's Movement

Foreword by The Rt Hon Baroness Seear

A Deirdre McDonald Book
Bellew Publishing
London

First published in 1989
by Deirdre McDonald Books
Bellew Publishing Co. Ltd.
7 Southampton Place, London WC1A 2DR

Copyright © by Ian McDonald 1989
All rights reserved

Colour photographs by Jonathan Watts

Designed by Bob Vickers

ISBN 0 947792 26 0

Printed and bound in Hong Kong by
Regent Publishing Services Ltd

Frontispiece: *At the end of the 19th century, women were seeking fuller lives and the 'New Woman' set the pace. As the next century dawned, postcards established themselves and chronicled women's progress.*

CONTENTS

Author's Acknowledgements

I would like to thank Lady Seear for the interest she showed in this book and for the trouble she took in writing a Foreword for it.

I am particularly grateful to David Doughan and the staff of the Fawcett Library for their help in identifying reference material and for allowing me access to postcards in the Library's possession. Similarly, I would like to thank Diane Atkinson and the Museum of London.

The team who produced the book itself deserve praise as well as thanks: Bob Vickers for the design; Steve West and Brian Gregory for the origination; Jonathan Watts for the colour plates; and Nancy Duin who checked the entire text. Most of all though I would like to thank my publisher who quickly understood the fascination of the postcards and who guided the project through its various stages to such a successful conclusion.

The illustrations in this book are of items in the author's own collection with the exception of No. 83 from the Fawcett Library/Mary Evans Picture Library. However, for use of illustrations still in copyright, the publishers and author gratefully acknowledge the following: Athena International; Bamforth & Co.,; Ed Barber; Syd Brak/Folio; Ian & Thalia Campbell/ U.F.L.O.E.; Oscar da Costa/Spitting Image; Dodo Designs; Jacky Fleming; Fi Francis; Fawcett Library; KQP Ltd; Annie Lawson; Kate Marshall/Junius Publications; John Minnion; Raissa Page; Private Eye; Jill Posener; Viv Quillin; Sue Sanders; Catrionia Sinclair; Southern Printers; Cath Tate, Chrissie Thirlaway; Mike Wells; Helaine Victoria. Special thanks to Leeds Postcards and Acme Cards for all their help and co-operation. Although every effort has been made to contact all copyright holders, the publishers would be pleased to hear from anyone they have been unable to trace.

FOREWORD

ARTOONS have for centuries provided sharp satirical comment on politics and politicians and have become part of our political vocabulary. Often highly sophisticated, they have hit their targets with deadly accuracy and they are an obvious and valuable source for historians, who have used them extensively.

The postcard has had no such status. It is seen at most as pop art, and primarily as an easy, and – once upon a time – a cheap way of keeping in touch with friends and relations – 'Having a lovely time. Wish you were here' has probably been its most familiar message.

The author of this book has recognised that in the past, and to some extent today, there was far more to the postcard than is generally realised.

As this book illustrates, cards have been used as a means of communicating a political or social message and so provide valuable material for historians. But their historical value is not limited to the evidence they provide of the views of various pressure groups. Unlike the cartoon, which is avowedly political in its purpose, the vast majority of postcards have been produced commercially to sell to the general public. That public is not in the main the public that chortles or rages over cartoons and writes letters to *The Times* about them. It is the vastly wider public that is looking for something to send to Mum and Dad and Aunty Glad, to Tom, Dick and Harry. So the postcard manufacturer has to ask himself what his market wants. What it wants, surely, is something which the sender thinks will amuse or excite the recipient or which expresses a view he strongly supports. So the manufacturer is taking a poll, as it were, of the public's views. If he gets it wrong, his cards won't sell. Seen in this light, postcards, like cartoons, can provide valuable historical material witnessing to the enthusiasm, the passions and the beliefs of the period in which they circulated.

This short history of the suffragettes and of the women's movement has been built round a remarkable collection of postcards, drawing on them

in a most unusual way as a historical source. Those specifically designed by women and their supporters for their own propaganda are obviously of considerable interest. But it is the commercially produced postcards which convey, in a way which would be hard to achieve in words, the feelings aroused by the women's movement and so the atmosphere the women had to endure. Contempt, anger, hostility, bewilderment are stamped on the cards. So, too, is the patronising attitude which has sometimes made women's ostensible supporters far harder to put up with than their uncompromising opponents. The postcards also bear witness to the naïvety of some of the enthusiasts as well as to their heroism.

It is the postcards that give this work its special cutting edge. But, even without cards, what a story it has to tell! The twentieth century has certainly been a century of revolution and of rapid changes, both peaceful and violent. Yet it can be argued that, of all the upheavals this century has experienced, none has affected more people more permanently than the changes that have taken place in the lives of women, who are, after all, half the human race. The release from incessant childbearing, the release through modern technology of endless domestic chores, the extension of education, the opportunity to earn money and to keep it – these do indeed constitute a revolution. Today, as never before, a woman is seen as a person in her own right and not only as a member of a family – a right expressed in the political equality won by the women whose struggle this book records.

To some, it seems the changes have come too slowly, that the benefits have been too unevenly distributed and that the world remains basically a man's world. Certainly there is much still to be done. But to look back, as this book does, to two hundred years ago, when Mary Wollstonecraft wrote *A Vindication of the Rights of Woman* is to realise how great the changes have been. The events traced in this book and the material it uses throw vivid light on some of the most important phases of that onward march.

Nancy Seear

Caswall Smith photo

MRS. HENRY FAWCETT L.L.D.
PRESIDENT OF THE NATIONAL UNION OF WOMEN'S SUFFRAGE SOCIETIES

Millicent Fawcett (1847-1929) campaigned throughout the whole of her adult life for the emancipation of women. This postcard, taken from a photograph in 1913, is smaller than the normal size and was likely to have been produced by the NUWSS.

INTRODUCTION

THE women's movement first took root during the last years of the 18th century and had its first flowering in the parliamentary debates of the 1860s and 1870s. Picture postcards are less deeply bedded. Their seeds were sown by the Continental cards of the 1870s and 1880s, and although pictures appeared on cards in Britain towards the end of the 19th century, it was not until January 1902, when the Post Office allowed a full picture on one side of a postcard, that their use became widespread.

The Edwardian era rapidly became the Golden Age of picture postcards. Publishers poured out series after series; new photographic and printing techniques produced quality cards at cheaper prices; advertisers, private organisations and publicists embraced the new medium; and an ever-growing army of collectors gleefully sent them through the post or lovingly preserved them in albums. The women's movement shared in and contributed to this enthusiasm. Their activities prompted cards – often very uncomplimentary – from commercial publishers, and their own propagandists seized the chance of gaining publicity. At the moment when the confrontation with government reached its climax, both women suffragists and picture postcards displayed their finest colours.

From 1904 to 1914, the postcards provide a contemporary commentary on many of the events of the campaign for women's votes. It is a record seen partly through the eyes of the general public and partly through those of the campaigners themselves. The pictures have an immediacy which brings alive the vitality of the moment and creates more vividly than words the fervour of those times.

The women's cause was overshadowed by the emergencies of World War I, but by their active support for war work, women demonstrated far more effectively than by argument the justice of their case. Postcards stayed with them. They give us pictures of women at war, sharing the burdens of the nation and standing equally with men.

Thereafter, but for totally unrelated reasons, the women's cause and postcard production follow a similar pattern. With the vote won, women began to enter Parliament. More gains were made: the voting age was lowered, and women shared in government. Strangely no celebrations or demonstrations reminiscent of the pre-war years marked these achievements. It was as if the women, sharing the status of men, had not found a land fit for heroines. Postcards, too, never recaptured their golden days. The use and styles of postcards continued but much of the originality had gone. Perhaps the public preferred the better illustrated magazines and found novelty in telephones and radios. Whatever the reason, postcards welcomed the new women in a manner more muted than in Edwardian days but more suited to the postwar mood.

Women's involvement in World War II was almost taken for granted. Of course they could do war work. After World War I why not? Little thought seems to have been given to the women left alone facing civilian aerial attack and struggling to bring up children on limited incomes and rationed goods. Postcards show them alongside men in patriotic poses or with a glamorous seaside cheekiness. The use of postcards themselves declined. There was no great mass of troops encamped in trenches for months, waiting for and writing the daily postcard. After the war the decline continued as cinema and television took the public's imagination and postcard publishers lost their originality. In spite of political change, the postwar years witnessed a return to traditional attitudes. The turmoil of war gave way to a search for stability, and after years of uncertainty, the woman's place was seen once again as being in the home. As reconstruction progressed, the consumer society seemed to offer ample compensation.

But in the 1960s something stirred. A postwar generation of women began to ask questions; questions about the world and about themselves. The rights of women had not been fully won. The hopes of the Victorian leaders had not been fulfilled with the granting of adult suffrage, and women still encountered numerous examples of injustice and inequality. Their reaction was universal and became the women's liberation movement. Coincidentally postcards were rediscovered. The charm of

Edwardian days was recreated in films, on TV and in books, and this engendered a popular nostalgia. Postcard albums retrieved from attics revealed pristine cards rich in chromolithographic tints and all the insouciance of *fin de siècle* Europe. Gradually interest in postcards revived. Collectors sought them, they appeared in books, and publishers tentatively revised and refreshed their designs. Postcards again became a form of popular art and entertainment. With them have come the independent publishers – artists, photographers and propagandists. Members of today's women's movement, like their Edwardian forebears, have been quick to produce some telling cards of their own. We can buy them now – radical, unsettling, provocative.

This book is not a comprehensive history of the women's movement but rather a selection of postcards relating to the movement and presented in a way which enables them to be seen in their historical

1. *The prescience of Edwardian postcards – One year out – Margaret Hilda Thatcher became Prime Minister on 3 May 1979.*

Meeting of Cabinet Ministers 1978.
Mrs Spankhurst, M.P., delivering her maiden speech.
728

"Automatic Suffragette Exterminating Pillar-Box"
(patent NOT applied for).

2. *To draw attention to their cause, suffragettes set fire to letter boxes, ignoring the anger that they aroused among those who had lost their mail, and paying even less regard to subsequent generations of postcard collectors. Postcard publishers took little direct action to restrain the women from destroying the products on which their businesses depended. No doubt they assumed that ridicule would sell more postcards.*

context. Naturally this means that in some instances – particularly in the 19th century – the coverage is sparse, but by using other pieces of printed ephemera, it has been possible to provide continuity. In this way, the book will be of interest to the general reader as well as to those with specialised interests, whether they be committed feminists or postcard collectors.

The postcards themselves provide a unique view of the events as they happened and may thus be seen as historical documents which have received, as yet, only limited attention. They are a tribute to the women whose sacrifices and perseverence helped to advance their movement to the position it enjoys today.

1

THE PIONEERS

MARY WOLLSTONECRAFT'S *A Vindication of the Rights of Woman* invites comparison with Thomas Paine's *The Rights of Man* published only one year earlier in 1791. Paine – the 'godfather' of the American War of Independence, a participant in the French Revolution, and secure in the advantage which men had in determining their own future – wrote of the 'nature and quantity of government proper for man'. His book sold over 1.5 million copies but is hardly read now. Mary Wollstonecraft – daughter of a despotic drunkard and weak mother, sketchily schooled, and with a sister and a friend let down by men – first spelled out the tribulations of woman. Her book remains a seminal work.

She wrote not simply of woman's exclusion from government and of her lack of rights in education, property and justice, but of the way in which society is moulded by a man-made environment in which woman is denied the chance of being her true self. She identified the distinction between feminism and femininity – the latter being a concept acceptable to men – and she reached the kernel of the difference between women and men in their sexual relationships. These issues are alive today.

They were not so readily received in her own time. She had supporters – publishers, writers and a public following – but in the hurly-burly of those years there was little revolutionary fervour left for women. Her own independent lifestyle – she had an illegitimate daughter by the American writer Gilbert Imlay – deterred other women from following her lead. Even women writers, practising a skill in which women's ability to excel had already been recognised, drew back. This was also true of the next generation of women writers. Harriet Martineau, for example, whose early success lay in popularising political and economic questions, felt that Wollstonecraft lacked control and had given in to self-indulgence. Martineau's own approach was to find the facts, analyse them and present a reasoned argument while keeping her emotional life out of her work. Hannah More and Sarah Ellis practised a similar dichotomy and other women writers often felt a conflict between their work and their lives. But the brilliance of Victorian women's writing, evinced by such names as Mrs Gaskell, the Brontës, George Eliot and Elizabeth Barrett Browning, displays the extent to which the views and feelings of women were being examined and brought before a larger public.

Women's education

One thing that all of these women agreed on was the importance of education. Emily Davies, to whom more is owed on this subject than to anybody else, went so far as to distance herself from the suffrage campaign so that any involvement in it would not prejudice her chances of making progress in the availability of education. Her attitude was simply that the more women were educated, the more they would be able to win their rights, including the vote.

A major step in this direction was the opening of Queen's College and Bedford College in, respectively, 1848 and 1849. Originally intended to train governesses – one of the few recognised careers for women – they rapidly developed into providing wider education of incalculable value to women and the women's movement. Of equal significance was the recognition that girls' education should not be limited to matrimonial needs. Two women helped lay the foundation for girls' secondary education: Frances Mary Buss, who founded the North London Collegiate School in 1850; and Dorothea Beale, who became Principal of Cheltenham College in 1858, four years after its creation.

Emily Davies secured the right of girls to take the recently instituted Oxford and Cambridge local examinations and, in the face of resistance from the universities, started her own college at Hitchin. Later, moving just two miles from Cambridge, she founded Girton College and, when the modest Newnham College was set up, she held out for examinations based on the university papers. With her students successful, the way was open for women's colleges to expand.

Improvements in education could do little immediately to alleviate the injustices being suffered

3. *Robert Burns, who died in 1796, still found time amid the confusion of the new republican era to recognise the position of women and to write the couplet reproduced on this postcard.*

> *Amid this mighty fuss just let me mention*
> *The rights of woman merit some attention*

It is also worth a little attention that comic postcards, revelling in the excitement of the women's campaign, could, after more than 100 years, echo the words of Mary Wollstonecraft.

Dorothea Beale, LLD.

4. *After a single year at Queen's College, Dorothea Beale became one of its tutors in mathematics and then taught for a year in Casterton where she was exposed to the shortcomings of traditional methods. On becoming Principal of Cheltenham College, she set standards which others were to follow. In 1864, she was responsible for the preface to the official report of the Girls' Education Commission. She wrote extensively on educational, historical and literary matters and earned an international reputation. Edwardian postcards recognised the achievements of Victorian women.*

by women, and by the 1850s, an increasing number were seeking to free themselves from the constraints under which they lived. However, suffrage reform was not yet seen as the central issue. Emily Davies was not alone in thinking that progress could be made through the existing system, and when the law was at fault, some women challenged it.

Married women and the law

In 1826, Caroline Norton faced the break-up of her marriage to the Hon. Richard Norton, who had treated her violently, and the loss of her three children

to whom he had denied her access. They were a well-connected couple. She was the grand-daughter of Richard Sheridan and on friendly terms with Lord

Melbourne and the leading Whigs – but she had no rights. By law, the husband owned all his wife's property – even any money she might earn – and had legal rights over the children. Richard Norton went as far as to bring a lawsuit against Lord Melbourne for advising his wife, and although the case was dismissed, Caroline Norton was publicly humiliated. For ten years, as a woman with no means or legal status, she fought on, publicising her predicament and gaining support from friends, lawyers and other women who had similarly suffered. In 1837, she met Mr Talfourd, a lawyer and MP who was attempting to introduce an Infants Custody Bill. They worked together, survived further scandals, and in 1839 the Infants Custody Act, which gave mothers rights to their children, became law.

Caroline Norton's case had been won at terrible cost to her own life, but she and her supporters had succeeded in changing the law and it provided others with an example of all that needed to be done.

Barbara Leigh-Smith – who later became Madame Bodichon – was one such person. As a young woman, backed by her father and some of his lawyer friends, including Talfourd, she prepared a *Brief Summary in Plain Language of the Most Important Laws Concerning Women* outlining women's legal disabilities. It gained support, was backed by a petition signed by 26,000 men and women, and Sir Erskine Perry turned its thesis into a Bill proposing that property rights and the power to make wills should be extended to married women. In Parliament, it clashed with the Marriage and Divorce Bill and, in 1857 after the normal wrangling with pressure groups, religious interests and the parliamentary timetable, the latter took precedence. This Act made major improvements in the rights of divorced women to retain their property, have custody of their children and receive payment for future maintenance, but male privilege was upheld by allowing a man to divorce his wife for adultery while a woman required further grounds such as cruelty or desertion. And married women had to wait thirty-five years for their property rights.

Early feminists

The first feminist meeting of 1855 is also credited to Barbara Leigh-Smith, and she was closely associated with the influential Langham Place Group – a number of independently-minded women. From this small beginning, more and more women came together with a common purpose. Some of them were writers, including Anna Jameson who also founded the *Englishwomen's Journal*; others went out lecturing; and one group set up the Women's Employment Bureau to assist a new generation of women seeking a different place in society.

Josephine Butler made an outstanding contribution. A woman of intense moral and religious conviction, she had worked among the poor in the slums and docksides of Liverpool where her husband was Principal of Liverpool College. Here she encountered the appalling circumstances in which so many women lived, and when controls over prostitution were introduced, she saw how callously they were treated by the law. After years of neglect, the government sought in the 1860s to limit the spread of venereal diseases by a series of Contagious Diseases Acts which gave the police powers to accuse women of being 'common prostitutes' and thus force them to undergo medical examination. This was clearly a gross violation of civil liberties: refusal to comply was punishable by imprisonment whereas acquiescence meant that a woman's reputation was lost.

Agitation against the Acts spread. The Acts themselves and amendments to them had been hidden from debate in the House of Commons; the police and local authorities were allowed to act in secret; and there were no trials. In addition, since the purpose was to prevent infection in the army and navy, why was no action taken against the men?

Josephine Butler led the protests with verve, but she had to contend with the attitudes of women as well as those of men. To talk of prostitutes and sex was just not done in polite Victorian society, and many women turned away from such unsavoury subjects. Some saw Mrs Butler as an extremist, but she had no hesitation in continuing. She created a furore by confronting the government candidate in a notorious by-election in the garrison town of Colchester where she and her supporters faced constant attacks from mobs. At the ensuing Royal Commission, she was the only woman to give evidence among the massed ranks of army and naval officers, doctors and lawyers. After this commission and other committees had sat and pondered and the arguments had gone to and fro, and when finally Parliament was reconsidering the Acts, she hired a hall in Westminster and filled it with women kneeling in prayer.

His latest purchase.

5.   *It was not until 1882 that a Married Women's Property Act gave women the right to hold property in their own name. However, old habits died hard, not every woman would want to take her husband to court. This hand painting was sold in the 1890s as one of a series by 'Cynicus' the pseudonym of the Scottish artist Martin Anderson, who was later to produce many postcards. Like Burns, he felt a natural affinity with ordinary people, but his pictures often record human conceits and deceits. He could have a cruel crayon despite his kind heart.*

"Strangers yet"

6. *Towards the end of the century, women had come to realise that the injustices to which they were subject could only be resolved by having voting rights on a par with men. The law itself was one of the greatest impediments they had to overcome. Martin Anderson, who was a strong supporter of the infant Labour Party and drew many pictures decrying the wrongs of capitalism, sympathised with the women's cause. However, he saw everybody as figures of fun and his postcards often show women in a poor light.*

The Close,
Winchester

My dear Friend
I do hope you will
be left quietly in prison for a
time   In these days
we must esteem a prison
dress a real honour

J E Butler

7. *This image of Josephine Butler is taken from W. T. Stead's* 'Portraits and Autographs' *published by his* Review of Reviews. *In a note, he explains that photographs of her did not give as good a likeness as this bust. The 'autographs' are excerpts of letters he received from her when he was in prison: 'My dear friend, I do hope you will be left quietly in prison for a time' and 'In these days we must esteem a prison dress a real honour'. J. E. Butler*

Although her campaign against the Contagious Diseases Acts was not backed by the whole of the suffrage movement, she would not have been out of place among the later militants.

The Acts were suspended in 1883 and repealed in 1886.

She aroused far greater public support for her joint action with W. T. Stead, the editor of the *Pall Mall Gazette*, against the 'white slave traffic' in young girls. The scandal of the buying and then selling overseas of girls over the age of thirteen had been known for some years but no action had been taken. Mrs Butler made public accusations in Brussels and was challenged to produce evidence. She enlisted Stead's help, and with the aid of the Salvation Army, he contrived to buy a girl of just thirteen and take her to a reformed brothel keeper with whom she stayed overnight. The following day the girl was sent to Paris and put into the care of a Salvation Army officer. Stead

8. *W. T. Stead went to prison for the part he played in stopping the 'white slave traffic' in young girls. For his newspaper articles, he had purchased a girl from her mother, but his opponents had him convicted on the grounds that the legal 'owner' was the father – a Charles Armstrong. Later it emerged that Armstrong was not the father and that only the mother's consent had been needed. Stead had served three months, but this did no harm to his outstanding career as an international journalist.*

This photograph was produced on thick card by the London Stereoscopic Company which later went on to produce postcards when the postal regulations allowed. Stead also produced postcards in association with Evelyn Wrench. He died on the Titanic, *sailing as one of the distinguished guests on its maiden voyage.*

Yours truly,
William T. Stead

LONDON STEREOSCOPIC CO   PERMANENT PRINT

then began to serialise the story in the *Pall Mall Gazette* under the title 'The Maiden Tribute to Modern Babylon'.

It scored instantaneous success. The public saw sex, smelled scandal and delighted in vicarious condemnation. Stead was attacked for his part in the affair and for using it to sell his journal. But as the instalments appeared, they were increasingly read and, blowing the dust off the Criminal Law Amendment Bill, untouched for five years, the government hurried it through a second reading. The public outcry continued unabated and the Bill became law in less than a month.

Although a supporter of women's suffrage, Josephine Butler acted independently from the suffrage movement. Indeed, her activities had embarrassed many of its leaders, some of whom had accepted that some form of control over the spread of venereal diseases was necessary, and it was only the method that needed to be changed. Others feared that the nature of her campaign would make it more difficult to win public support for theirs. Some members of the women's liberation movement of the 1960s and 1970s, however, have seen in Butler's tactics of working through pressure groups and public demonstrations lessons which could still be applied.

The suffrage societies

The claim for women's suffrage had gathered pace by the mid-19th century. The first debate in the House of Commons on women's right to vote had come immediately after the great Reform Bill of 1832. Ironically, the claim was based on property – under which laws most women were severely disadvantaged. The intrepid Miss Mary Smith of Stanmore in Yorkshire had property and considerable wealth – but no husband. Since voting rights for men were determined by ownership of property why should she be excluded? The Radical 'Orator' Hunt put her case and pointed out that she was subject to the law but could not share in making it, and – shades of the American War of Independence – since she paid taxes, she should be allowed to elect a representative. The debate degenerated into the ribaldry which so bedevilled so many of the arguments on women's rights, but this case is of more than historical interest since it embraces a number of themes which were to re-emerge throughout the next 100 years.

Anti-suffragists were to argue that married women's interests were protected by their husbands' votes. Did women want special protection for spinsters who, later research has shown, made up 13 per cent of the female population and who had little chance of earning a living? And if property was to play a part in determining voting rights, how could the franchise be extended to more people as most Liberal politicians wanted? Such questions would haunt a suffrage movement made up largely of married middle-class women.

A much more straightforward argument was the Quaker view advanced by Anne Knight, that women should simply be treated equally with men. She published this in a leaflet in 1847 and sustained it

through the Sheffield Association for Female Franchise. This concept was held by a number of women, but there were few organisations to propagate their views.

A breakthrough came in 1865 when John Stuart Mill, the eminent author of *Principles of Political Economy* and *Treatise on Representative Government*, was invited to stand for Parliament by the City of Westminster. He even referred to the extension of voting rights to women in his election address. The Langham Place Group were over the moon. They raised money, formed a support committee and revelled in the fun of electioneering. Their volunteer efforts did his cause no harm, and on his election, women had a champion in the House of Commons.

In the same year many leading women – Emily Davies, Barbara Leigh-Smith, Dorothea Beale, Frances Mary Buss, Elizabeth Garrett (later Garrett Anderson) and many others – formed a discussion society in Kensington. At an early meeting about fifty women voted in favour of political activity.

Their commitment and preparedness was timely, for in 1866 politicians were talking of further parliamentary reform. Barbara Leigh-Smith asked Mill what advice he might have and he suggested that the women might organise a petition which he could present. They went at it with a will. A committee was formed – the first women's suffrage committee – and within a matter of weeks, Emily Davies and Elizabeth Garrett were able to present Mill with over 1,500 signatures which, as he said, he could 'brandish'. More were collected through groups in Manchester and Edinburgh, so that by the time the Election Reform Bill was debated in May 1867, more than 6,000 further names had been added.

Mill later said that his contribution to the parliamentary debate on women's suffrage had been his 'most important public service'. For the first time, the issue had been dealt with seriously. His own speech was one of the clearest statements explaining the position of women – ' . . . the confiscation of one half of the species . . . whose interests are confined within four walls . . . Who are as unrepresented by their husbands and brothers as workpeople are by their employers . . .' – and it fired the whole of the movement. But Parliament felt it already had enough on its hands. The government's priority was to extend the franchise – and this meant men. The new Bill used the word 'man', which could be interpreted as less restrictive than the term 'male persons' found in the 1832 Act; Mill simply suggested that the word 'person' alone should be adopted. He gained over 70 votes in support of this amendment, but the majority hesitated, resisted change and possibly feared for the future.

Mill's other great service to women was the book he published two years later, four years before his death in 1873. *The Subjection of Women* stands with *A Vindication of the Rights of Woman* as vivid statements of women's case. Mill had an outstanding academic and literary reputation, but his commitment to the women's cause had been inspired by his wife. He had been devoted to her and had seen the world through her eyes.

One immediate result of his efforts was the spread of women's suffrage activity beyond London and particularly to Manchester, where Lydia Becker had set up a suffrage committee to help with the petition. She was one of the first women to see parliamentary reform as the key issue in advancing women's rights, and she devoted her energies entirely to this end. For more than twenty years, she was totally involved in organising groups, tirelessly speaking at meetings, producing countless pamphlets, briefing sympathisers in the House of Commons, and giving the movement a single-minded sense of direction. The scale of her work can be seen in her magazine *The Women's Suffrage Journal* in which she details every relevant parliamentary speech and the minutiae of suffrage societies' meetings.

She had an early opportunity to show her paces. In 1867, the name of Mrs Lily Maxwell had been accidently included in the list of voters for a by-election in Manchester. Amid the general interest and amusement which this aroused, Lydia Becker helped Lily Maxwell to record her vote. She followed this up by organising hundreds of other women to get their own names recorded in the electoral register. At this point it became a legal question and the young radical barrister from Manchester, Richard Pankhurst – whose wife's later achievements have inevitably overshadowed his own – was ready with the arguments. He had recently published an article in the *Fortnightly* journal arguing that, under the 1867 Election Reform Act, women were entitled to vote and, when the women's cases came before the High Court, he acted as junior for Sir John Coleridge QC. The case was lost but, undaunted, Lydia Becker immediately sent letters to every parliamentary candidate asking for their support for a Bill to establish women's suffrage.

This was the type of organisation and campaigning that built up the suffrage societies. Committees soon spread around the country with Edinburgh, Bristol and Birmingham in the lead. Women spoke at public political meetings – something that would have been unthinkable in mid-Victorian days – first, Lydia Becker at the Manchester Free Trade Hall in 1868, and then Millicent Fawcett in 1869 in London.

Women were also making their marks on other walks of life. The charitable work of Louisa Twining and Angela Burdett-Coutts was recognised, and in 1870, women rapidly exercised their right to serve on the new school boards. Soon some became poor law guardians and municipal councillors. Elizabeth Garrett had become the first British woman doctor and was helping other women to enter the profession.

Such achievements undoubtedly helped the suffragists who continued to lobby at Westminster. During the 1870s, they succeeded in getting parliamentary debates in every year but one, and fuelled by facts and opinions from Lydia Becker, MPs had no excuse for being ill informed. The main political parties, however, provided no leadership, seeing women's suffrage as a matter of conscience for individual members. Disraeli spoke in favour of women voting but did nothing more about it. Gladstone was even more ambivalent. Unfortunately, too many Members saw these debates as an opportunity for flippancy, and many others, though silent, were opposed.

Lydia Becker used every opportunity to raise the question of extending the franchise. She worked with MPs to bring in Private Members' Bills – one of the most helpful was Jacob Bright, Lily Maxwell's constituency MP– and whenever constitutional matters were to be discussed, she ensured that the women's argument was heard. She gained some successes throughout the decade. The majority of 123 against Mill's amendment to the 1867 Bill declined to well below 100, but by 1879 it was back to 114.

THE SUFFRAGETTE
Nails her Colours to the Mast.

Votes for Women

While in the act of voting, Mrs Jones remembers that she has left a cake in the oven !

9. & **10.**   *The concept of the combative female suffragist is a theme in early Edwardian postcards. It is surprising how many of these seem to have been inspired by Lydia Becker, showing women with steel-rimmed spectacles, piled up hair and sporting Tyrolean type hats, reminiscent of those worn by Becker's German father. Postcard artists of the time may have remembered her from Victorian cartoons. Leaders of the movement were conscious of the adverse effect that such cartoon caricatures could have, and at meetings were at pains to seat some of the younger members in prominent places on the platform or in the audience.*

BRITISH ORDER OF DISTINCTION FOR WOMEN · 1883·

IN DORSETSHIRE.

Fair Cyclist: " Is this the way to Wareham, please?"
Native: "Yes, miss, yew seem to me to ha' got 'em on all right!"

FROM "PUNCH."

11.   Top: *This postcard commemorating the creation of the
'British Order of Distinction for Women' demonstrates that
women's increasing role was being recognised. The Order was of
little direct benefit to the women's movement however.
Significantly it dates from 1883, the year that the Corrupt and
Illegal Practices Act had authorised volunteer workers to take
part in electioneering – and who could do this better than
women? In 1885, the Primrose League provided a place for
women in the Conservative Party, and the Women's Liberal
Federation came into being two years later. Women's interests
were thus divided into splinter groups.*

12.   Above: *The invention of the bicycle gave the 'new woman'
freedom to travel and a sense of liberation.
It called for special dress and the American suffragist Amelia
Bloomer devised the garment that bears her name, but later she
abandoned it fearful that the attention it received would detract
from her work as a feminist. Postcards could not resist the jokes:
Fair Cyclist: 'Is this the way to Wareham, please?'
Native: 'Yes, miss, yew seem to me to ha' got 'em on all right!'*

The 1884 Reform Bill

At the 1880 general election, the Liberals were returned and, with them, so the suffragists thought, a majority in support of female suffrage. The work of the suffrage societies was bearing fruit, and at the Liberal Party Conference there had been a large vote in favour of further constitutional reform which included votes for women. These high hopes were dashed when a new Reform Bill was published. It made no reference to women's rights and, when an amendment to this end was proposed, it was rejected by the leadership.

The precise reasons for this are difficult to adduce, but they include some of those that had already defeated women's suffrage Bills plus a few new ones. Gladstone was no ardent supporter of women's suffrage. His priority in the Reform Bill was to extend voting rights to a larger part of the population, albeit male. If he were to include women, the Bill might fail completely. The majority in his party who favoured votes for women did not constitute a majority in the House of Commons. Gladstone may also have thought that women voters might prove to be more conservative than men and thus present a long-term threat to the Liberals' future. This hard-headed approach to politics cannot be ignored, but neither should Gladstone's similar stance against Private Members' Bills when less was at stake.

This setback undoubtedly disappointed the suffrage societies. Like mountaineers scaling a peak, they had breasted what they thought was the final ridge only to see further peaks beyond. They would press on, fortified by the experience, but conscious of all the unclimbed hills ahead. There were signs that their path would be even trickier. Both of the major parties set up special women's sections, thus creating a division along party political lines. This had an immediate impact on the suffrage societies, many of whose members were closely identified with, and worked through, the Liberal Party. In 1888, the Central Committee of the suffrage societies split in two; one half (the majority) worked with the Women's Liberal Federation, and the minority, including Lydia Becker and Millicent Fawcett, continued on non-party lines. Worse was to come: in 1889 a number of leading women, including the novelist Mrs Humphry Ward

and the socialist polemicist Beatrice Webb, published a *Protest Against Women's Suffrage*. In spite of prompt ripostes from the women's movement, their enemies had gained more ammunition.

The saddest loss at this time was the death of Lydia Becker in 1890. It was she who had welded the suffrage societies into an effective force and who had managed the parliamentary links. A Lancastrian but with a German father, she was a woman of many interests – as a botanist, she had corresponded with Darwin, and she had launched a literary and scientific society – but she had realised her vocation in her work for the women's cause. It was she, too, who had borne the brunt of much of the public argument. In an age when women hesitated to attend public meetings, much less speak at them, she could command an audience. With her steel-rimmed spectacles, her hair in a bun and her rotund figure, she was a gift to caricaturists and was lampooned cruelly, becoming the prototype of the dominant academic woman seeking her rights in a masculine society. It is a measure of her influence that her image was still in the minds of postcard artists over ten years after her death, but one could wish that she might have had a kinder memorial.

At the time of her death, women had reached a point that would hardly have been imagined fifty years earlier, with many having taken up positions that would not have been open to them. Some outstanding women had brought about fundamental changes by their individual efforts. Women's rights had been recognised in Parliament – and sometimes granted. Their role in national affairs was already being accepted.

But the movement lacked cohesion. There was no agreement on priorities nor any co-ordinated action to achieve objectives. It was a movement with many strands. Some, such as Emily Davies and Josephine Butler, pursued particular goals; others, such as Lydia Becker, saw women's rights devolving from Parliament; and still others simply wished to free themselves from the injustices which inhibited their everyday lives. They had laid a foundation on which, despite temporary setbacks, they and subsequent generations of women would build.

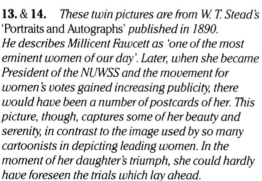

13. & **14.**   *These twin pictures are from W. T. Stead's* 'Portraits and Autographs' *published in 1890.*
He describes Millicent Fawcett as 'one of the most eminent women of our day'. Later, when she became President of the NUWSS and the movement for women's votes gained increasing publicity, there would have been a number of postcards of her. This picture, though, captures some of her beauty and serenity, in contrast to the image used by so many cartoonists in depicting leading women. In the moment of her daughter's triumph, she could hardly have foreseen the trials which lay ahead.

Philippa Fawcett crowned Emily Davies' efforts to secure higher education for women when, in 1890, she sat the mathematical tripos at Cambridge University. As the daughter of such renowned suffragists as Millicent Fawcett and Professor Henry Fawcett MP, she epitomised the hopes of the women's movement. Not only did she pass but was placed first. Mathematics, which requires a logical approach to abstract concepts, had long been regarded as beyond the capabilities of women. Her achievement routed many detractors and was rated more highly even than that of Miss Clifford from Girton who gained a first in classics.

2

THE EARLY CRUSADES

MILLICENT FAWCETT was only twenty-two years old when she spoke at a London suffrage meeting in 1869, and she lived long enough to witness, in 1928, the year before her death, the enfranchisement of all women aged twenty-one and above. Her precocity in political and public affairs is partly explained by her family background. Her father, Newson Garrett, was something of a radical conservative and encouraged his five daughters to act for themselves. All of them became active in the women's movement. One, as Elizabeth Garrett-Anderson, became the first female doctor in Britain, and Millicent, six years years her junior, saw her and Emily Davies take the petition to John Stuart Mill in 1866. The following year, Millicent married Professor Henry Fawcett who, as a Liberal MP, became Gladstone's Postmaster General.

After Lydia Becker's death, Millicent Fawcett became more and more involved in running the Central Committee, which remained unaligned to any political party. It is easy to imagine her discussing with her husband the pros and cons of being linked to the Liberal Party after the 1884 débâcle. Henry Fawcett had abstained from voting and, as a member of the government, had incurred Gladstone's displeasure but had not been asked to resign. She would also have talked it through with Lady Frances Balfour, the sister-in-law of Arthur Balfour, Conservative Leader of the House of Commons and a future Prime Minister. When in 1897, the divergent societies reunited as the National Union of Women's Suffrage Societies (NUWSS), Millicent Fawcett became President and Lady Frances a leading committee member. In the following years, regional societies (including a separate one for London) completed the reorganisation.

Further encouragement also came in 1897. Faithful Begg, a Conservative stockbroker from Glasgow, backed by an impressive petition of over a quarter of a million signatures which bedecked Westminster Hall, introduced a Private Member's Bill for extending the franchise to women. On its second reading, it won a majority of 71, by far the best result since 1884. Although opponents took the now time honoured course of blocking the Bill by talking it out so that it did not reach the committee stage, it showed that considerable underlying parliamentary support did exist.

Women's employment

One of the criticisms levelled at the Victorian feminists was that they comprised no more than a handful of comfortably off, well-educated women. The irony of the Langham Place Group's Women's Employment Bureau assisting independently minded young women from middle-class families while thousands of working women toiled in appalling working conditions for indefensibly low rates of pay will be obvious to anybody interested in the forces of political change. The feminist leaders were conscious of the needs of working women but had not found the means to help them. Millicent Fawcett would have been fully aware of the situation because of her husband's direct involvement in women's working conditions.

In 1873, the government had set up an inquiry into factory hours. The time worked by women had been limited to ten hours a day under the Factory Act of 1847 which was designed to protect women and children at work. Men could work without restrictions. The women's movement saw this as another example of discrimination against them since men could earn more money and benefit from overtime. Leading Liberals, believing in the freedom of the individual, resented that women should be made to suffer because of restrictions imposed by law, and Henry Fawcett presented the women's case in the House of Commons but without success.

Part of his case was that women should protect themselves through trade unions as men did, and Emma Patterson, who had begun the work of setting up women's unions, also endorsed the view that they

Wigan Pit Brow Girls.

15. Left: *The outcry in 1842 against the way in which women were forced to work in mines resulted in their being excluded from such employment. Women continued to work on the pit brow, shifting and loading coal, but in 1887, they feared that they might lose their jobs as a result of legislation limiting the weight that they could be asked to carry. When medical reports showed that this could be detrimental to health and child bearing, one of them told the Home Secretary: 'I ha' had fourteen children, sir, and I never was better in my life.' They kept their jobs. Today, in a number of countries, women work in coal mines.*

16. Below left: *Sisters of the pit-brow women were the shore-based workers of the fishing industry. In most ports they sorted, gutted, packed and carried fish. They made good subjects for postcards which show the dockside scenes and the distinctive costumes of different regions. Like that of the pit-brow women, their work would decline in the years to come.*

17. Below: *One of the most rapidly growing occupations was office work. The new typewriters and telephones required skills that women eagerly offered. The 1890s – the naughty '90s – saw women realising that they could earn a few shillings to break free of routine domestic life. This was an ideal subject for comic postcards – 'Things at the office are so pressing, shall be late home' – and they made the first jokes that recur to the present day. Now it is recognised as a form of sexual harassment.*

Lowestoft Fishing Industry—Packing Herrings.

Things at the Office are so pressing, shall be late home!

should be free from legal constraints. This was, in fact, an over-simplification. Hours of work and rates of pay needed to be improved for all workers; male trade unions resisted the membership of women because of the low pay that they were prepared to accept; and working men themselves wanted improved conditions of work and would not be averse to protective legislation. Emma Patterson continued to campaign within the Trades Union Congress (TUC) for equality of treatment until her death, when others, such as Mary MacArthur who founded the National Federation of Women Workers, took up the struggle.

Millicent Fawcett was herself involved in another instance which demonstrated the gap between political attitudes and the realities of life for working women. When the government reviewed the regulations for the mining industry in 1887, she escorted a delegation of pit-brow women to see the Home Secretary. They were afraid that regulations which aimed to protect their health by limiting the heavy work they undertook would result in them losing their jobs. An astonished Home Secretary listened to their arguments, and the regulations were dropped.

Cases such as these, together with the growing strength of the Labour Party, no doubt reinforced Millicent Fawcett's belief that the women's movement should remain free from political affiliation.

Such incidents are small in relation to the rapid growth in women's employment towards the end of the century. Regardless of whether women as a whole supported the suffrage movement, there was undoubtedly a vast number seeking a way of life unknown to their mothers. By the early 20th century, women made up almost one third of the working population – nearly 5.5 million altogether. Some were in traditional occupations but the growth had come from new industries, some of which, such as nursing and school teaching, had been fostered by women themselves. Florence Nightingale's nursing school at St Thomas's Hospital changed attitudes almost as much as her work during the Crimean War had done. Initially she had had reservations about the women's movement, but as it matured, she lent her name in support.

In most industries, women fared badly in comparison with men. Pleased to have the chance of working, they readily accepted low pay and poor terms of employment. Often they worked in small enterprises – shops and offices – or on a part-time or temporary basis, all of which impeded improvement.

One area in which large numbers of women were permanently employed was the Lancashire cotton industry, and here they were also members of the relevant trade union. Although protected by it, they suffered financially in relation to male workers – women received five shillings a week compared to men's twenty-five shillings – but they could see no other method of improving their situation nor a way to link it to the women's cause. In the 1890s, however, two young women, Esther Roper and Eva Gore-Booth, started to explain to them how changes might be made.

Esther Roper was one of those dedicated workers who are often remembered by the organisations they have created. She was Secretary of the influential Lancashire and Cheshire Suffrage Society during its period of peak activity; Eva Gore-Booth, born of an Irish family, had a radical rebelliousness that was to prove to be even more potent in her sister (see Chapter 6). Between them, they roused the mill girls. A measure of their success is the petitions they sent to Parliament in 1901 and 1902 calling for votes for

18. *Postcard collectors will be fascinated by this photographic card of the Flamborough postwoman. The Post Office first tried to employ women in 1872, but male staff made such a protest that the experiment had to be abandoned. The following year, a more modest proposal involving only 11 vacancies was successful – but 2,000 women applied for them.*

O.H.M.S. The Flambro Postwoman.
Publisher
Wm.R.Readhead,Stationer
Flambro.

19. Top: *Teaching was one of the few professions in which women made rapid progress. Mary Carpenter's 'ragged schools' for poor children and her public work had paved the way. The new women's colleges trained young women as teachers, and despite some resistance, they became accepted. By 1911, the Census showed that in the lower 'professional grades', which largely comprised teachers and nurses, three times as many women were employed than men. This card depicts one school that was typical of the times: St Michael's Infant's School in Gloucester at the turn of the century, with the children wide eyed at the photographer, and their watchful teacher.*

20. Above: *This laundry, with only two men in sight, was the sort of small industrial unit which Emma Patterson found so difficult to unionise. The safety guards over the machines are something of which the company could be proud – they were by no means in general use in most factories, where the women's loose hair and long dresses would have been hazards.*

SERVANTS' INSURANCE ACT.

SERVANT'S INSURANCE ACT

BOVRIL CREAM. WINE

"I burnt my small toe and I don't mean to work till it is quite better, I prefer to have a burnt toe."

21. & **22.** *About 1.5 million women worked in domestic service – about one third of all working women at the time. This group (top) looks contented, but a bad employer or bullying butler could make life unbearable. Domestic servants had few rights. In the early 1900s, the Conservative government introduced compulsory compensation for industrial injuries, and following the Liberal victory of 1906, Lloyd George, then at the Board of Trade, extended this to cover domestic service. This prompted numerous cartoons of servants falling downstairs, being waited on in bed, or collecting their compensation. The women's movement does not appear to have been involved.*

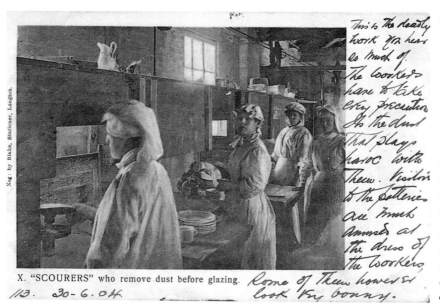

X. "SCOURERS" who remove dust before glazing.

23.   Even when women wore special clothing and worked in such closely knit communities as the Staffordshire potteries, there could be treacherous health risks. Messages on postcards can be illuminating. This one reads: 'This is the deadly work you hear so much of. The workers have to take every precaution. It's the dust that plays havoc with them. Visitors to the potteries are much amused by the dress of the workers. Some of them however look very bonny.'

THIS WEEK   NEXT WEEK

Oh wouldn't life be a grand success
With the pleasures that surround it,
If we hadn't to face the wretchedness
Of WORK, next week, confound it.

DAVID JAMES SHACKLETON. M. P.
COPYRIGHT PHOTO ELLIOTT & FRY.

24.   *The growth of the Lancashire cotton industry provided work for thousands of women. Mill girls divided their lives between the clogs and tea cans of the mill and breaks at home or seaside holidays. Their wages gave them little more than the chance to buy a few personal items. A century later, women still experience friction between their careers and their private lives.*

25.   *Thanks to women textile workers, David Shackleton became one of the Labour Party's first MPs. He was President of the Northern Weavers' Association and a member of the Blackburn Chamber of Commerce. In the 1906 general election, he retained Clitheroe with a majority of 8,207 and continued to support women's suffrage in the House of Commons. In 1910, he introduced the Conciliation Bill (see Chapter 4).*

women, for which they collected no fewer than 67,000 signatures from the cotton and textile workers.

In 1902, they made a more startling and much more significant breakthrough. At a by-election in Clitheroe, the women wanted to back a candidate of their own choice and used their majority in the local trade union to get money allocated to pay the expenses and salary of the Labour candidate David Shackleton. After a deal with the Liberals, he was given a clear run, and on his election, received yet another petition reminding him to press the women's

case. He did not let them down.

Elated by this success, sights were set on backing a candidate for the next general election. Their choice fell on Wigan, which had a Conservative member with a none-too-large majority. Again they backed a candidate jointly with the Labour Party, but textile workers were less powerful in Wigan than in Clitheroe and the miners' union gave their support to the Liberal. In a three-horse race, the sitting member was re-elected on a minority vote and the women had lost their bet. But by that time Mrs Pankhurst was on the scene.

Emmeline Pankhurst and the WSPU

If John Stuart Mill's devotion to the women's cause had been inspired by his wife, Emmeline Pankhurst's dedication owed something to her husband. Their lives had not been easy since Richard Pankhurst had acted with Sir John Coleridge in arguing that the 1867 Election Reform Act gave women the right to vote. He continued his legal career, but his political activities brought disappointments and possibly dissipated his energies. He stood for Parliament in 1883 and 1885 for the Liberals but lost on both occasions and, along with so many others, was disillusioned by the 1884 reform. A natural radical, he felt briefly at home in the Fabian Society and decided to run as an Independent Labour candidate for Gorton in Manchester at the 1895 general election. Again he lost and then, tragically, he suddenly died in Manchester in 1898.

The effect of her husband's death on Emmeline Pankhurst, coming after the frustrations they had shared, must have been immense. They had been a well-suited couple. She had complemented his intellect and radicalism with a Parisian education that embraced the commune of 1871 and showed itself in her comradely feeling towards her fellow women and men. They had moved from Manchester to London and back again in the course of Richard's political pilgrimage and for a time she had run a shop to help pay the expense of bringing up their four children, two of whom were now embarking on careers: Christabel, the eldest, studying law at Manchester, and Sylvia, art. Mrs Pankhurst herself then took a job with the Registrar of Births, Deaths and Marriages.

But she had learned a great deal from Richard and had seen political forces at work. Even if she could not agree with the reasons, she understood why Gladstone had turned his back on women's suffrage. Alongside Richard in Manchester, she had met the

Labour leaders and had begun to assess the possibilities of working through the Labour Party. She had grown impatient, too, with the methods employed by the suffrage societies. She saw the value of using Private Members' Bills but felt it unlikely that any of these would succeed without the backing of the major parties.

As her children grew up, she sought ways of using her pent-up energy and decided, in October 1903, to form her own women's organisation. At one point, it might have become part of the Labour Party, but she came to realise that its priorities, like those of the Liberal Party, would not necessarily be hers. Christabel helped her choose the name – the Women's Social and Political Union. The word 'Social' might have been included to attract the socialists, or to refer to a wider role beyond suffrage. No one knew and it did not matter. In the event, it became known by its initials – the WSPU.

It was immediately active in Lancashire and within the Labour Party. Mrs Pankhurst did much of the work herself, meeting people and speaking at meetings. Her daughters helped her as did Esther Roper and Eva Gore-Booth. Soon they attracted other workers, two of whom – Annie Kenney a mill worker from Oldham, and Teresa Billington, a former national organiser from the Independent Labour Party – would stay at the forefront of the campaign in the years to come.

As 1905 dawned and the prospect of the next general election appeared on the horizon, the hopes of the women's movement again began to rise. On 12 May, a sizeable group of women from the suffrage societies, and including Mrs Pankhurst and some of her members from the WSPU, went to the House of Commons to hear the debate on Bamford Slack's Private Member's Bill which decreed that in all Acts concerning qualifications for voting, words of the masculine gender should be held to include women. The women had hardly expected that their case would be greeted with enthusiasm, but they must have been incensed by their opponents devoting virtually all the available time to a puerile debate about rear lights for cars and horses. These were the tactics to which anti-suffragists such as the voluble MP Henry Labouchere had resorted for years. Was this how parliamentary democracy worked? A group of women left the house. As they gathered outside, Mrs Wolstenholme Elmy, almost the Victorian mother figure of the movement, was about to say a few words but was moved on by police. She tried later in another place and was again moved on, and even the intervention of the sympathetic Labour leader James Keir Hardie could not prevent the police from taking the women's names and addresses.

This may have been the moment when Mrs Pankhurst perceived the tactics that the women, in their turn, might employ to frustrate their adversaries. In her autobiography, she explains how Parnell's campaign for Irish Home Rule had impressed her. When her husband had contested the 1885 election and as a Liberal had supported Home Rule, he did not win Irish votes because Parnell had withheld his support from Gladstone's government. By making his presence felt, he exerted power. Could civil disobedience have the same effect?

In October 1905, as a prelude to the coming election, Winston Churchill had been adopted by a Manchester constituency following his conversion to Liberalism and held a meeting in the Free Trade Hall. After his exploits in the Boer War, he was already a well-known public figure and Sir Edward Grey, one of the leading Liberals had come to speak on his behalf. The Misses Christabel Pankhurst and Annie Kenney sat ready in the audience. When questions were invited, Annie Kenney asked Churchill if he would make women's suffrage a government measure. Although both he and Grey were known as supporters neither immediately replied, and Christabel jumped up with a 'Votes for Women' banner. In the confusion of the struggle that followed, both women were arrested and, having refused to pay a fine, were sent to prison.

The publicity they received more than compensated for the indignities and privations they suffered. The newspapers were full of it; not supportive, but the message was there. And when they came out of prison, there was Keir Hardie and a mass meeting at the same Free Trade Hall, with flowers and songs and crowds struggling to get in to the hall. Those who did shared an emotional bond forged by the two young women and, after Keir Hardie had spoken, they heard Christabel Pankhurst and knew that the movement had a young orator and another potential leader. Mrs Pankhurst, who had been in the Free Trade Hall when the fighting had broken out, must have felt that she could see the way ahead.

The position of the political parties

The election which took place in January 1906 was not about women's suffrage. It was about the vacillations of the Conservative government and their indecision as to whether tariff reform should replace free trade. The Liberals, as the heirs of free trade, also had a package of reforms directed towards helping the community at large. Neither major party mentioned women's suffrage. Indeed, looking at the array of electioneering postcards that candidates used, the public was evidently more concerned about the employment of Chinese workers in South African gold mines than they were about the status of women in the United Kingdom.

The parties seem to have effectively muzzled the question. The concept that votes for women was a matter of conscience for MPs still held sway, and neither Conservatives nor Liberals appeared willing to force the issue. Broadly speaking, the Conservatives were more generally opposed, although their leadership, from Disraeli to Salisbury, had been sympathetic. The new leader, Arthur Balfour, although personally in favour, acted as he did on most political questions and simply sat on the fence. In the Liberal Party the reverse applied. Here a clear majority of MPs backed women's suffrage and voted for it, but after Gladstone's hesitation, the Liberal leaders Lord Rosebury and Sir Henry Campbell-Bannerman seemed uninterested and the heir apparent, Herbert Asquith, cast himself in Gladstone's mould.

The women's sections within the major parties also appeared to have neutralised their women members. In 1891, when Millicent Fawcett had actually spoken and been well received at the Conservative Party Conference, the Primrose League had voted in favour of women's suffrage. Later they drew back, and this undoubtedly contributed to the revival of the suffrage societies. The pressure in the Liberal Party was more marked. In 1892, the Women's Liberal Federation, led

Our Women's Unionist Association

Our Women's Liberal Association

26. & **27.**   *At first glance, these two cards by 'Cynicus'
would seem to be like many others that poked fun at
the women's movement. But the captions reveal that
the joke is at the expense of the political parties whose
well meaning women members have been corralled
into women's groups which are doing nothing for
women's rights. This is what Lydia Becker and
Millicent Fawcett feared more than 15 years earlier. As
so often happened Cynicus liked being on the side of
the angels but could not help drawing like the devil.*

by the Countess of Carlisle, refused Gladstone's request to set aside the divisive issue of women's suffrage in favour of Home Rule for Ireland. A majority of the women left the Federation to set up a new organisation – the National Women's Liberal Association – and remained independent until after World War I. Nevertheless, within the Liberal Party, support remained strong and those remaining in the Federation had pushed for an end to discrimination in national and local elections in 1905.

One other political party must be mentioned: the Irish Nationalists who could count on about eighty seats. They used their voting strength solely to achieve their one objective – independence for Ireland – and thus had no interest in women's suffrage. When a government had a majority over all other parties, the Irish Nationalists' influence was negligible. When their votes were needed, they were powerful – as the women were to find.

28.   *Walter Crane, better known as an illustrator of children's books, was one of the idealistic middle-class Victorians who supported the Labour Party in its infancy. He drew a number of pictures for the Labour movement and some were reproduced as postcards. This one commemorates the Paris Commune of 1871 in which working women and men attained equality.*

JULIA DAWSON,
"The Clarion" and
"The Woman Worker."

29.   *Many British socialists adopted a more pragmatic approach to achieving their aims. The Clarion Clubs were active in trade union and Labour Party circles. Julia Dawson worked for* The Clarion *and no doubt agreed with its editor, Robert Blatchford, that women's suffrage might impede progress towards socialism: if women won the franchise, many might vote against socialist candidates, and socialism was the only means of bringing about true equality between all men and women.*

As for the diminutive Labour Party, what help could they possibly be? They were not much further down the political road than the women were. They also sought representation for their members and justice for the working class. The idealists among them wanted justice for women too, but there were others who asked what middle-class women could do for the workers? Were there really grounds for a common cause?

Against this mass of male inertia the women continued to exert themselves. Some progress could be claimed: the suffrage societies had recovered from the setbacks of the 1880s and were again an effective organisation; franchise associations had been established in the political parties and among specialist groups such as graduates and actresses; and in the House of Commons, in 1904, Sir Charles

" I don't know whether your eyes are better than mine, but when I first saw these loaves I was absolutely unable to tell which was the big one. I know there is a difference, because I know that in the smaller one a few ounces less flour had been used in order to correspond with the amount of the tax, but it is still, I think, a sporting question—which is the big one and which is the little one."—*See Mr. Chamberlain's Speech at Birmingham.*

30. & **31.** *Another card which appears to belittle women but is, in fact, satirising party politics. Joseph Chamberlain was the maverick politician of the turn of the century. Originally a Liberal, he joined the Conservatives and then almost split them on the issue of tariff reform. Having made the customary Liberal obeisance to women's rights, he changed his tune to become a leading anti-suffragist.*

In arguing for tariff reform, he used two loaves (above left) to show that the 'free trade' loaf and the 'tariff reform' loaf would be the same. This was manna from heaven for political cartoonists, and these loaves crop up in countless postcards.*

G. F. Christie, who drew the card above right, linked it to yet another ridiculous accusation directed at women – that their brains were smaller than men's. Chamberlain, still toying with his bread, tries to insinuate that the Liberals who support the women's cause are soft in the head, but the phrenological bust on the shelf behind cannot help laughing at him . . .

McLaren's resolution in favour of women's suffrage had gained a majority of 114. It was the best result since 1897, but as on other occasions, it had led nowhere.

Many women felt frustrated – not simply the little group that Mrs Pankhurst had gathered around her but also those who had come to her meetings or had felt the resentment of being moved on by police when they had wanted to talk outside the House of Commons. And there were those who, from the days of Josephine Butler, had been aching to do something more effective as well as those who had grown up since and wished to play their part in helping the movement. Already a distinction was being made between those who followed the lead of the suffrage societies by working within the law and those who felt that stronger action was needed. These two groups came to be called the 'constitutionalists' and the 'militants'.

How should the women's movement react to a majority of MPs who paid lip service to their cause but acted and voted in accordance with their own priorities? How could women deal with the politics of pressure groups, of bargaining and of power? And how could they handle the differences in their own ranks? Would they, as the men might suggest, fail to stay the course?

Yet, with the growing realisation of the scale of the struggle, more women were daily being better educated, seeking jobs, building careers and moving into a world in which they had previously had no place. Like a tide lapping up a sandy beach, it would slowly go on rising until it would engulf and level the man-made sand castles.

3
MILITANCY

THE women's hopes must have been sky high when the election results were announced in January 1906. The Liberals swept in with one of the largest-ever majorities – 399 seats to 157 for the Conservatives – and with Labour increasing their share from 2 to 29. Surely there must now be a majority for women's suffrage?

32. *Immediately after the 1906 election, Emmeline Pankhurst moved the WSPU to London. Since her husband's death, she had been ready to take decisive action. She created and embodied the suffragette spirit and was quite prepared to sacrifice her own life. Many of her colleagues resented her autocratic style and few could match her fanaticism. A statue of her, unveiled on 6 March 1930 by Stanley Baldwin, now stands in the gardens next to the Houses of Parliament.*

MRS. PETHICK LAWRENCE.
JOINT EDITOR OF "VOTES FOR WOMEN."
HONORARY TREASURER, NATIONAL WOMEN'S SOCIAL & POLITICAL UNION.
4, CLEMENTS INN, W.C.

MRS. PANKHURST.
HON. SECRETARY NATIONAL WOMEN'S SOCIAL AND POLITICAL UNION.
4, CLEMENTS INN, W.C.

BY MARTIN JACOLETTE, SOUTH KENSINGTON.

33. *In addition to being Treasurer of the WSPU, Emmeline Pethick Lawrence co-edited the journal* Votes for Women *with her husband. They worked almost as one person, and in the spring of 1906, their flat at 4 Clement's Inn,(the address on these postcards) became the organisation's headquarters. Later, proper offices were taken in the same building. Like the other leaders, Emmeline Pethick Lawrence was an eloquent speaker and courageous campaigner. Her first experience of a Black Maria shocked her: expecting to find seats like those in a bus, she was caged in a tight individual compartment. Worse was to follow.*

There were other heartening pointers. The WSPU descended on London and, from a standing start, were able to assemble 300 women at a meeting in Caxton Hall to mark the opening of Parliament. Many of them had come from the East End where Sylvia Pankhurst had been building contacts. When the meeting heard that the King's Speech did not mention women's suffrage, Mrs Pankhurst led them to lobby the House of Commons. Refused entry, they continued their demonstration outside No. 10 Downing Street to announce their arrival to the Prime Minister.

They also gained two outstanding converts who were to share with the Pankhursts the future development of the WSPU. The Pethick Lawrences brought administrative efficiency to the organisation. Emmeline Pethick was the independently minded daughter of a wealthy West Country family; he was a Fellow of Trinity College, Cambridge and a former President of the Cambridge Union. They had both

been active in social work, and their joint name marked their mutual respect. Mrs Pethick Lawrence became Treasurer of the WSPU early in 1906 and her husband provided close support and an extraordinary ability to raise money. He well appreciated that, as a man, it would have been out of place for him to play a leading public role, but he was constantly available as a writer and counsellor.

It soon became apparent that the election had brought no fundamental change. The ever-enthusiastic Keir Hardie – who had helped Annie Kenney and Sylvia Pankhurst organise the Caxton Hall meeting and had introduced the Pethick Lawrences to Emmeline Pankhurst – had seized an early opportunity to raise the question of women's suffrage in the House of Commons. On 25 April 1906, the

34. *Keir Hardie had long supported the women's cause. He saw it as a straightforward injustice which could be corrected in a straightforward way. After his election in 1892 as the first Labour MP, he had taken his seat to the sound of a trumpet and wearing a cloth cap. He was the new way. He had brought the various socialist and industrial groups together to form the Labour Representation Committee. In the 1906 election, with the triumph of 29 MPs and almost as many more who had run as Liberals, he was ready to help women to do the same.*

35. *William Randal Cremer, the Labour MP from Shoreditch, had an impressive international reputation. He had worked in the shipbuilding industry and for many years had been Secretary of the International Arbitration League. In 1903 he had won the Nobel Peace Prize. He opposed women's suffrage as an irrelevence to the growth of socialism and international harmony. In 1907 the Labour Party patched up this internal division by opting for a policy of universal adult suffrage but, as a result, almost caused Keir Hardie to resign.*

1856. Keir Hardie 1906.
G. C. Beresford, Photo.]

WILLIAM RANDAL CREMER. M. P.
COPYRIGHT PHOTO ELLIOTT & FRY

'Ladies' Gallery' was packed with women who heard another Labour MP, William Cremer, attack the resolution with all the tired old arguments of men's responsibilities, women's emotions, and his own tender feelings towards the opposite sex. He was followed by other members with similar views seeking to talk the resolution out. The WSPU women, who were less inured to this type of thing than their elders in the NUWSS, created something of a disturbance, and with time running out, began to call for a division. Police who had been standing by immediately expelled them and no vote was taken. They may have got nothing from Parliament but at least they got publicity.

Some of it was harmful. The NUWSS was inundated with complaints about the unseemly behaviour of the militants and began to distance themselves from them. This led to more friction as, with the help of over 200 MPs, they had been arranging a delegation to see Sir Henry Campbell-Bannerman, the new Prime Minister, and naturally the WSPU wanted to be represented.

Eventually a delegation was agreed which brought together the suffragists and other women's groups – from graduates to textile workers, co-operative workers to members of temperance groups. Emily Davies led it, but despite her forty years' experience of such meetings, she could not budge the Prime Minister. He accepted the suffragists' arguments and confirmed his own sympathies for them, but said that his government was not in a position to do anything. Annie Kenney, in spite of promises of good behaviour, called out, 'Sir, we are not satisfied!' and none of the women disagreed with her.

The WSPU was going to do something about it. They felt that Asquith, the new Chancellor of the Exchequer, was their principal opponent in the Cabinet and thought that Campbell-Bannerman's comments had confirmed this. Emmeline Pankhurst went to heckle him at a meeting in Nottingham but was unceremoniously ejected. Next they planned a protest at his London house. On 21 June, Teresa Billington and Annie Kenney led groups of women through the elegant streets to 20 Cavendish Square. Stopped by police, there was a tussle and four suffragettes were arrested. The trial at Marylebone Police Court caught the headlines. Teresa Billington refused to accept the magistrate's authority since he was applying man-made laws. Nevertheless, she was fined and, refusing to pay, went to prison as did the others. But her outburst could not be confined, and judging by the number of comic postcards that reproduce the event – the slight figure of a woman in the dock in a male-dominated courtroom – the public

36.   *One example of a 'man-made law' was the Deceased Wife's Sister's Bill, which was passed by the House of Commons with large majorities no fewer than 13 times but was always rejected by the House of Lords. The purpose of the Bill was to legalise a marriage between a man and his deceased wife's sister. Although not exclusively related to women's rights (the women's movement played little part in the extended legislative process), it typified the obstructive capability of the Lords and the law-making role of men. Even when it was finally passed in 1907, the Peers Spiritual opposed it and forbade the clergy to solemnise such marriages.*
This postcard is by a thoughtful young Donald McGill, free of his seaside ribaldry.

A LANCASHIRE LASS IN CLOGS AND SHAWL BEING 98
"ESCORTED" THROUGH PALACE YARD.

CHORUS

Take me back to Palace Yard, Palace Yard, Palace Yard, that's where I long to be
With the friends so dear to me: the tall policemen smiling, bland, to gently take me by the hand,
For "Women's Rights" anything we will dare: Palace Yard, take me there'

37. *This card is probably from a photograph taken outside the House of Commons during the demonstration against the failure of W. H. Dickinson's Bill in March 1907. Groups of working women from Lancashire and Yorkshire had been brought down to London for the occasion. It marks a significant change in postcards of the movement by showing the involvement of working women and the authority of the police.*

It is also an example of the way in which new photographic printing techniques could be used on postcards to record news-worthy events. It was postally used in June 1907, and the sender, who is having 'a fine old time', might well have been a supporter.

loved it. It also paid off in the House of Commons, where MPs asked questions about the severity of the sentences, especially considering the advanced age of some of the women.

A demonstration in October provoked an even greater outcry. The WSPU had begun the practice (which they were to continue in the years ahead) of holding a 'Women's Parliament' to coincide with the opening of Parliament. Already their ranks were swelling: in addition to Emmeline Pethick Lawrence, Charlotte Despard, who was well known for her social work in South London, and Mary Gawthorpe, a school teacher and leading socialist from Leeds, were among the 200 women at the Central Hall, Westminster. They soon got news that the government had no intention of introducing legislation for women's suffrage in the coming session. Women jumped to their feet in instant protest, and the police moved as quickly to maintain order. In the scuffling that followed, Mrs Pankhurst was knocked to the ground, some women attempted to reach the entrance of the House of Commons and ten were arrested. In court the next day, they were fined £10 but, on refusing to pay, were sentenced to two months' imprisonment.

The severity of the sentences rather than the scuffles claimed public attention. The courts and the government had seen no way of dealing with the women other than by imposing the harshness of the law. In prison, instead of being seen as political, 'first division' prisoners, they received 'second division' treatment: they were allowed no privileges and were forced to wear prison clothes. Too late the government realised its mistake. Reductions in sentences and improved conditions could not disguise their ineptitude. This reinforced the conviction of the women and allowed them to reassert their unity. *The Times* was ready to print a letter from Millicent Fawcett in which she wrote:

I hope that the more old-fashioned suffragists will stand by their comrades who in my opinion have done more to bring the movement within the region of practical politics in twelve months than I and my followers have been able to do in the same number of years.

The women had survived their baptism of fire and emerged the stronger.

Charlotte Despard and the Women's Freedom League

The year 1907 was busy but difficult – busy because support for the movement grew so rapidly, and difficult because the women still disagreed among themselves and men proved yet more fickle.

It even rained on what came to be called the 'Mud March'. This was the first major demonstration organised by the NUWSS and, despite the bad weather, showed the scale of support that they could muster. On a dank February day, more than 3,000 women of all ages and walks of life marched with

Now Madam _ Will you go quietly or shall I have to use force?

"I protest against Man-made laws".

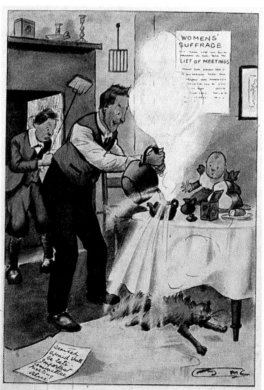

The Suffragette <u>not</u> at home.

Well I'm ————

"What are men, who are they, where are they, &c.&c."

above one of the crowd.

But surely my good woman don't you yearn for something
beyond sufficient money to provide you with your immediate
needs, doesn't your heart swell with the thought of elevating
your sex to a share in making the laws of your country?
"I aint got no time mum."

38-43. *This set of cards is by the well-known political cartoonist Arthur Moreland. Some of them repeat the traditional jokes of dominant women running meetings – the Tyrolean hat persists – and the popular theme of inept husbands left at home to get the meals and look after the children.*

The picture of the suffragette in the dock protesting against 'man-made laws' draws directly on Teresa Billington's stand against the magistrate at her trial, and thus dates the set to the latter half of 1906. Her case undoubtedly caught the public's attention and echoes of it can be found in a number of postcards. Perhaps the women's movement did not make enough of the popular appeal that this argument might have had.

The hand of the political cartoonist can also be seen in the last card:

'But surely my good woman don't you yearn for something beyond sufficient money to provide you with your immediate needs; doesn't your heart swell with the thought of elevating your sex to a share in making the laws of your country?'
'I ain't got no time mum.'

Canvassers from all political parties still receive such replies.

44. & 45.   *These postcards did the cause an injustice, but with the women's organisations disagreeing among themselves, it is hardly surprising that postcard publishers did not always get it right. The 'suffragists' were the original supporters of women's suffrage – and included many men. They were organised through the NUWSS and acted constitutionally. 'Suffragettes' was a name coined by the press to describe militant supporters, and was applied to members of the WSPU and the Women's Freedom League. Early militant action such as the demonstrations outside the Commons brought benefit to all three organisations. After 1911, the public began to react against it.*

some apprehension through London from Hyde Park to the Strand.

Some days later, a WSPU meeting ended in violence. Charlotte Despard, leading a deputation to the House of Commons, was confronted by mounted police who rode down the marchers. The women re-formed into ranks time and again. Fighting continued for some hours until Charlotte Despard and many others were arrested.

These scenes shocked sympathetic MPs. One of them, W. H. Dickinson, promptly introduced a straightforward Bill to enfranchise women by eliminating the concept of gender in all Acts concerning voting rights. It reached a second reading by 8 March, but once again the opposition paraded the old arguments and those whom the women had thought were in a majority faded away. Millicent Fawcett, again writing in *The Times*, took them to task for not fulfilling promises of support given 'lightly and casually' at election time.

The women were not deterred. They mounted another demonstration, and this time used Caxton Hall not just as a meeting place but as a base from which to gain entry to the House of Commons. They were repulsed as before but only after prolonged fighting and many arrests.

As a character, Charlotte Despard seemed to have stepped straight out of fiction. From a wealthy family, she was a member of the Independent Labour Party; despite being the sister of a General, she was a pacifist; renowned for her work among the poor, she was sometimes regarded as a revolutionary. It is hardly surprising that, after two months in Holloway, she had views on what might next be done. Unfortunately, Emmeline Pankhurst did not agree with her.

46. & **47.** *The Women's Freedom League found postcards a useful way of establishing its identity. Not only was the WFL quick to appoint its officers but also to set up offices at 18 Buckingham Street, just off The Strand. Later it moved to 1 Robert Street by the Adelphi. It was also quick to use its strong provincial network by mounting a special campaign in Scotland.*

The founder of the WSPU was now driven by a single-minded vision. She ran the WSPU autocratically and wanted only her backers on the committees. She saw herself as engaged in a war where democratic processes had no place. After tedious resolutions and votes by the membership, the two women parted company in the autumn, and Charlotte Despard and her supporters, who included Teresa Billington and Edith How Martyn, founded the Women's Freedom League (WFL).

There were now three women's organisations active in the field: the NUWSS, built on the original concepts of Lydia Becker and run by Millicent Fawcett; and the two militant groups. The level of support for all three fully justified their separate identities. The NUWSS, by far the biggest, grew from 16 affiliated suffrage societies in 1903 to over 300 by 1911. The WSPU had 35 branches in London – the centre for most of its activities – but only 54 outside; while the democratic WFL had 64 provincial branches. Each organisation published its own magazine: *The Common Cause* from the NUWSS; *Votes for Women* (which had become the popular rallying cry) from the WSPU; and *Vote* from the WFL. As for funds, Millicent Fawcett estimated that the NUWSS handled over £40,000 per annum in the years

Miss **ALICE SCHOFIELD**
(Organiser)
WOMEN'S FREEDOM LEAGUE.
Offices—18, BUCKINGHAM STREET, STRAND, LONDON, and 30, Gordon Street, Glasgow.

Miss ANNA MUNRO, Secy. Scottish Council, 30 Gordon Street, Glasgow.

before World War I, and the WSPU with a much smaller base succeeded in raising between £20,000 and £30,000 each year. Frederick Pethick Lawrence, running the equivalent of an Edwardian telethon, would coax contributions from packed meetings by chalking up the totals on a blackboard. Allowing for inflation, the women's movement was as well endowed as the minor political parties of the 1980s.

All three organisations had the same objective: to secure the franchise for women on the same terms as men. They differed only on the means of obtaining it. Millicent Fawcett had long set the NUWSS the target of creating in each parliamentary constituency a women's suffrage society which would bring pressure on all parties when selecting MPs. To the militants, this was not enough. They wanted to bring direct pressure on government by whatever means they could. And for those women who found Emmeline Pankhurst's style too extreme, Charlotte Despard and her colleagues gave them a means of expression.

Earlier that year Christabel Pankhurst had urged her members, as they waited to attack the House of Commons, to 'seize the mace' like Cromwell. Would they now have the discipline of his New Model Army?

The heat of battle

They got off to a cracking start. At the opening of Parliament, the WFL tried to petition the King, and a Miss Matters, 2,500 feet up in a balloon, showered London with leaflets. Edith New and a nurse, Olivia Smith, chained themselves to railings in Downing Street. They and Flora Drummond – known as the 'General' and who had joined Emmeline Pankhurst in the Manchester days – were arrested and sent to prison. The NUWSS had a formal meeting with Asquith to learn from his own lips that he saw no chance of legislation without the approval of a general election, but the constitutionalists steeled themselves against this disappointment by putting their hopes on yet another Private Member's Bill to be introduced by Henry Stanger.

The new battlefield, though, was a string of by-elections. A number fell due in 1908 as MPs gaining ministerial posts had to seek re-election. Emmeline Pankhurst determined to oppose government candidates at them all, putting Parnell's policy into practice – attacking the party in power wherever it could be hurt. This was not easy for many of the suffragists to accept since their allegiance lay with the Liberal Party, but the WFL – despite the recent split – lent valiant support, particularly in Charlotte Despard's South London fief of Peckham where the government candidate was turned out. The Liberals in the constituencies found this tactic much less easy to accept, and in Mid-Devon, where in January the Liberal also lost his seat, his supporters were so incensed at the suffragettes' intervention that they caught Emmeline Pankhurst, rolled her in the mud and, but for the police, would have pilloried her further. She was still limping in February 1908 when, during a three-day Women's Parliament in the Caxton Hall, and after the police had already made fifty

Oh, what a Difference!
1. Reception of a Constitutional Deputation
to the British Parliament at Westminster   2. Its result

48. *This card, one of a series, was also apparently sponsored by the WFL. The suffragette is thought to have been played by Edith How-Martyn, one of its founders. It is interesting that the card stresses the reception of a 'Constitutional Deputation' as if militancy is being forced on women, in contrast to Mrs Pankhurst's provocative tactics. The WFL operated between the constitutionalism of the NUWSS and the extremism of the WSPU.*

PLENTY OF ROOM.

THE BOX-OFFICE ATTENDANT : "I'm afraid the seat you want is booked, sir, but there are plenty more from which you can get a full view of the stage."

Mr. CHURCHILL : "I'd rather have my old one, you know ; but it doesn't matter much so long as I can find another."

(If Mr. Churchill is beaten in North-West Manchester on elevation to Cabinet rank, there are safe seats for him elsewhere.)

49. *Churchill, having been promoted to the Cabinet, had to offer himself for re-election in his North-West Manchester constituency. This cartoon from the* Manchester Evening Chronicle *of 10 April 1908 aptly portrays the situation. A woman bars the way, but Churchill remains unflustered, knowing that he will be offered a safe seat. It was that rare combination of Eva Gore-Booth and Esther Roper who actually stood in his path. They roused a Barmaids' Association against the Liberal Licensing Bill, which would have prohibited the employment of women as barmaids, and, by joining with the brewers, they helped to reject the party of reform. Churchill, sympathetic to women's suffrage, took it all in good part.*

arrests, she led a deputation to Parliament, riding in a cart. She in turn was arrested and sentenced to six weeks in prison. She said she enjoyed the rare tranquillity.

Winston Churchill was another by-election victim, but he bore the women less malice than his fellow Liberals in the West Country.

The women could tweak the government's tail at by-elections, but in Parliament they could do little – and less still when, in April 1908, Asquith succeeded Campbell-Bannerman as Prime Minister. Asquith, with his patrician style, may have been the outstanding member of what has been described as one of Britain's most brilliant Cabinets, but he saw no place for women in politics. He could give loyalty to Campbell-Bannerman, let Lloyd George take the lead, and encourage the young Churchill, but he could not understand what women might do. He relished their company, but in private not public life. His reserved manner made him one of the least well known of the Edwardian political leaders. Postcards of him are

Taxation without Representation.

THE RETORT COURTEOUS.

Woman Taxpayer. "I wish to speak to you, sir, about the spending of my money."

Chancellor of the Exchequer. "Madam, all you have to do is to pay." *(Aside to Police)* "Chuck her out."

Printed and Published by the Artists' Suffrage League. 259 King's Road, Chelsea.

JOHN HAMPDEN.

Copied from Statue in House of Commons.

Women's Tax Resistance League,
10 Talbot House,
St. Martin's Lane, W.C.

Copyright]

Jane Bull: "No women admitted! No. wonder the place is in such a state. High time for a good Spring clean!" (Knocks)

Published by the **SUFFRAGE ATELIER.**

50. & 51. Above: *The argument that, because women paid taxes, they should have the right to vote was a very powerful one. It dated back to the 17th-century Ship Money tax and to John Hampden – 'who, with dauntless breast, the little tyrant of his fields withstood' – who in refusing to pay the tax contributed to the outbreak of the English Civil War. This argument was also a direct cause of the American War of Independence. The Artists' Suffrage League published a number of propaganda postcards for the movement; the one above, showing the hated Asquith as Chancellor of the Exchequer, must date prior to April 1908 when he became Prime Minister. The Women's Tax Resistance League, set up in 1909, grew out of the WFL. Its members stoically refused to pay their taxes, and bailiffs confiscated their belongings. Charlotte Despard's furniture was often seen at auctions.*

52. Left: *The Suffrage Atelier also produced propaganda postcards. This one, with a rather simplistic argument, was published in 1909.*

usually head and shoulder portraits showing an expressionless face like that of a member of a minor royal family or an insignificant visiting head of state. Compared with Joseph Chamberlain or David Lloyd George, of whom postcards abound, he is seldom seen. Yet in the propaganda postcards produced by the women's movement – and there are not a great number of them – Asquith features far more than anyone else. The women knew the man they had to beat.

With summer came not battles but parades. In two great processions, women displayed with style the strength of the movement. Women from all three organisations took part in both since many were members of more than one. The first, on 13 June, was organised by the NUWSS, who had had their members stitching and embroidering brilliant banners, each representing a group of women workers, a locality or whatever other reason had brought them together. They marched behind their banners – 13,000 strong and led by Emily Davies and Millicent Fawcett – from the Embankment to the Albert Hall.

Eight days later, on Sunday, 21 June, came the turn of the WSPU. They had publicised the event well in advance spending as much as £1,000 on advertising and special trains. To attract more people, there were seven separate processions converging on Hyde Park, where bugles sounded and the cry 'Votes for Women' swept across the crowds. Half a million

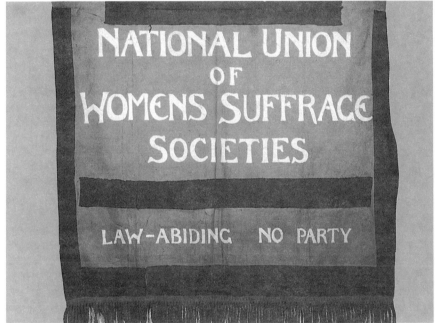

HYDE PARK DEMONSTRATION, SUNDAY, JUNE 21, 1908:
MRS. PANKHURST, MRS. WOLSTENHOLME ELMY.

53. *Some of the banners used in the processions have recently been reproduced on postcards from photographs by Ian Campbell. As well as providing an eye-catching means of showing allegiance, the banners gave some members a way of contributing to the cause. Women who may have found canvassing too arduous discovered that designing and sewing the banners allowed them to play their part. The NUWSS do not seem to have made as much use of postcards as the other organisations did.*

54. *The two processions of 1908 drew great crowds in the streets and publicity in the press. They provided a formula that was used in subsequent years. Although hundreds of thousands of people were involved, both as participants and as spectators, there was no violence and the police had little difficulty. The government remained unimpressed.*

people attended the demonstration, and although many of them might have been families simply out to see the sights, there could be no doubt that Londoners knew that the women had been in town.

Hostilities resumed at the end of the month with scuffles outside Parliament and the ugly involvement of youths posing as police. They frog-marched the women and let them fall forward on to the paving stones when released. Edith New, accompanied by Mary Leigh, again showed originality and courage by throwing stones through the windows of No. 10 Downing Street.

A morose autumn followed the summer. The industrial worker still saw no promised land but knew that unemployment was increasing. Parades of the unemployed and hunger marches touched more sensitive nerves with the general public than did the grievances of women. Attempting to widen their social appeal, the WSPU mounted a public meeting in Trafalgar Square, calling for popular support by 'rushing' the House of Commons. They had gone too far, and Emmeline and Christabel Pankhurst, and 'General' Drummond were arrested for breaking the peace. The women went further and linked their arrest to a Caxton Hall meeting for the opening of Parliament. Once again, the battle raged with the police, who made yet more arrests.

Their Bow Street trial brought the contestants face to face. The women had succeeded in having subpoenaed Herbert Gladstone, the Home Secretary, and Lloyd George as witnesses. Christabel Pankhurst,

drawing on her legal training, cross questioned them with the pertinacity of a Portia. Emmeline Pankhurst drew on her experience of politics, arguing (as so many extremists had done) that the court was not competent to try political cases: 'We are here not because we are law breakers; we are here in our efforts to become law makers.' Her words had little effect: she and 'General' Drummond were sentenced to three months in prison and Christabel to ten weeks.

The trial attracted wide publicity, just as the Pankhursts had hoped. Herbert Gladstone, who had been much criticised for allowing the harsh penal treatment of women, was thought to have acquitted himself well. No doubt he had thought his policy through. Lloyd George, the natural champion of the underdog and a known supporter of women's suffrage, had been far less at ease. Bound by loyalty to the Cabinet and burdened with the responsibility of office, he could not speak as the radical he had once been. Later that year, at a meeting arranged by the Women's Liberal Federation at the Albert Hall, it was possibly with relief as well as satisfaction that he was able to announce that the Prime Minister had made women's suffrage an open question for the party and the Cabinet, and that 'without imputation of disloyalty to his chief or his colleagues', he would vote for female enfranchisement in the Electoral Reform Bill to be submitted to Parliament.

Emmeline Pankhurst in her prison cell – she was released just before Christmas – must have wondered what his words might portend.

The limits of force

Women now committed themselves to the cause with the self-sacrifice of missionaries entering an alien land. They would volunteer at the WSPU's headquarters at Clement's Inn to undertake missions that the Union felt would achieve publicity or put pressure on the government. They accepted demonstrations, fighting and imprisonment without demur. They undertook with zest daring assignments – hiding in meeting rooms, chaining themselves to railings and accosting public figures. Emmeline Pethick Lawrence, the chief-of-staff of the WSPU, was herself arrested on 24 February 1909 at a march on the House of Commons. On her release from prison, the banners of the movement – recalling the processions of the previous year – greeted her like flags unfurled in military honour.

Lady Constance Lytton, a daughter of a former

Viceroy of India, and sister of Lord Lytton, joined the WSPU in January 1909. In her thirties and with some private means, she had been seeking active involvement in some worthwhile public or social work. She had met some of the WSPU leaders at a working girls' holiday school and had been impressed by their sincerity. Already interested in prison reform, she attended a suffragette breakfast to welcome back the released prisoners. She wrote to her aunt:

The moment of their coming out was thrilling. The prison doors, then a kind of courtyard to the gates, then the crowd outside. They simply ran out, rather dazed, and looking like children, some with their arms outstretched. The mixture of extreme joy and heart-tugging for those still left inside was very overcoming.

On the fringe of the Union, she had been outraged by the Bow Street trial, had tried to intercede for the

I want my Vote!

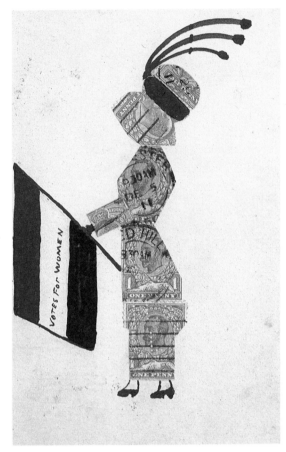

Do Women Want the Vote?

55. Above: *The WSPU colours of purple, white and green gained widespread recognition and were often used to represent any aspect of the women's movement, militant or otherwise. White signified purity; green, hope; and purple, dignity or loyalty. This was one of the most popular postcards – cats always had great appeal but, as this card would remind recipients, they could also scratch and bite.*

56. Above right: *Some postcard collectors enjoyed making pictures by sticking used postage stamps on plain postcards. In the absence of purple stamps, this enthusiastic supporter of the WSPU had to resort to using coloured ink. A woman dressed in red and green on a white background would be immediately recognisable as a member of the NUWSS. As the women's groups grew, so the colours proliferated. The Women's Conservative Union, for example, chose blue, white and gold, and the Suffrage Atelier the exotic blue, orange and black. No doubt all the colours looked splendid in the processions.*

57. Right: *Another fashion was postcards written in code. This one is simple – you just hold it up to a mirror.*

TO MEN ONLY!!

GREAT CLEARANCE SALE OF

SALE **LADIES** *SALE*

Some shop soiled, some been on the shelf
many years, some spoilt by mildew.

REMARKABLE LINE IN SUFFRINGETTES.

Suitable for street work and cell cleaning, warranted violent,
fond of bread and water.

AN ASTONISHING BARGAIN.

Several Musical Comediennes, with reputations rather the
worse for wear. Patchwork Morals, guaranteed not straight
laced. Very suitable for the Peer.

GIBSON GIRLS—Remarkable Figures in this Line.
Solidity cannot be guaranteed. Unbreakable. Remarkable
Advertisers.

Great Opportunity! a nude departure, licensed
by the L.C.C. - only one "mile-oh"!!

Now on show at the Palace. Recommended now for STEADy
men. The One and Only.

Very Special Line in Plain Figures for every day use

Only a few quiet, gentle girls, of the old sort we read about.
Warranted solid and steady all through. The son will not
fade them. Very suitable for wives and mothers.

Also a Job Assortment at giving away prices,
Of Lady Travellers, Lady Clerks, Cabdrivers, and
others in all ages. No use for housework.

Don't miss this chance.   This week only.

Note the Address:

TUMPTY & Co., 13, Always Avenue.

No. 208.

58. *Cards in the form of announcements were a regular form of political humour. This one is more offensive than most but is unusual in being solely concerned with women. It is particularly noteworthy in that it harks back to the campaigns of Josephine Butler and W. T. Stead of the 1870s and 1880s.*

defendants, and was won over by Emmeline Pankhurst's speech. Now she was ready to make a similar commitment. In this, she was typical of many women of that time; she was untypical in that she came from an aristocratic background and had personal contacts with public figures.

She was first arrested on 24 February and imprisoned for a month. The day after her release, she wrote another letter to her aunt:

Yesterday was one wild rushing excitement. Today I have been tired beyond describing. My brain refuses to work or take in anything. But I long to see you and be held tight in your soft loving arms and to explain some things to you. Holloway has been the greatest, most wonderful experience of my life. How I long to tell you things that have burnt into my brain and heart for ever. I know it may all be very boring to other people.

This sense of an almost religious conversion was not uncommon among members of the militant societies.

Lady Frances Balfour, who was President of the London Society of the NUWSS, went to a Caxton Hall meeting of the WSPU when yet another another deputation was being sent off to attempt to see the Prime Minister. She wrote about it to Millicent Fawcett, the NUWSS National President:

June 29th 1909

My Dear Mrs Fawcett,

I am just back from a night with the militants; Lady Betty and I went to the Caxton Hall first. The speeches were of a very serious nature, almost like a service of dedication. There was no excitement; we were all asked not to move as the deputation left the hall, to remain seated in silent thought for three minutes, and then to follow and cheer our comrades.

. . . We slowly battled our way up to Whitehall; here we saw several arrests, the women all showing extraordinary courage in the rough rushes of the crowd around them . . . The police kept us all moving . . . B. and I stood on the Treasury steps watching the crowd slowly driven up by a wedge of police . . . two women in front of us threw stones at the windows. A policeman had his arm round their necks before we could wink. Crowd and police made a rush together and B. and I were knocked flat falling in rather an ignominious heap! I was afraid the crowd would fall over on us . . . the two women were swept away with incredible speed . . . The courage that dares this handling I do admire. We saw one tall girl driven like a leaf up and down Whitehall . . .

Only days later, Marion Wallace Dunlop took self-sacrifice one step further to escalate the tension. Having been imprisoned, and apparently without any instructions or guidance from the WSPU, she refused to eat. Offered tempting food and drink, she turned aside all blandishments, and within a few days, starved but exultant, she was released.

Immediately other imprisoned suffragettes adopted the same technique. The officials at Holloway and other prisons did not know how to deal with them. Neither did the government. Then, in September, they took a fateful decision which perhaps many ministers came to regret – to apply forcible feeding. Mary Leigh, who had been imprisoned for attacking a meeting in Birmingham addressed by Asquith, became the first woman to endure the treatment.

Lady Constance read and heard of the sufferings of the women who had become her friends and to whose cause she was now committed. She knew that protests were being made in Parliament but having little effect. On 8 October, she journeyed to Newcastle, knowing that Lloyd George would be speaking there, and threw a stone at Sir Walter Runciman's car. Arrested, she ensured that she would be punished by emphasising her intent. Along with her comrades, she was sentenced to one month's imprisonment. She starved herself but was released on the 13th because of a weak heart.

Her adventure attracted attention but no great concern. Indeed, some said that she had received special treatment because of her rank. MPs who had

59. *'Lady Conny' won the hearts of the suffrage campaigners by exposing the shameless methods of the forcible feeding policy. After her ordeal, she renewed her pledge to continue fighting for the movement. Her actions saddened her mother, but she received strong support from her brother Lord Lytton and her sister Lady Betty Balfour. She considered that her heart condition – which in prison had been detected when her aristocratic status was known but ignored on another occasion when she was disguised – was not too serious. Nevertheless she was later struck down by paralysis, although it was never claimed that this was directly linked to her having been forcibly fed.*

LADY CONSTANCE LYTTON PHOTO BY LAFAYETTE, GLASGOW.
WOMEN'S SOCIAL & POLITICAL UNION
4 CLEMENT'S INN STRAND W·C·

been attacking the government's policy of forcible feeding now asked if all of the women prisoners were being given heart tests. The government resisted them stubbornly.

On 14 January 1910, in the middle of a general election and unbeknown to anyone, Lady Constance resolved the question of preferential treatment in her own way. She disguised herself as a seamstress – coat a little too short and with suffragette badges on the lapels, spectacles and a drastic haircut – and took part in a protest meeting outside Walton Gaol in Liverpool where it was known that forcible feeding was taking place. When arrested, she gave her name as Jane Warton and was sentenced to fourteen days' hard labour. She refused food, was given a cursory medical examination, pronounced fit and forcibly fed. It was some days before the authorities realised that something was amiss. They contacted the Home Office and the news of her identity was out. She was quickly released but she had won her point.

By 31 January she was well enough to address a women's meeting at the Queen's Hall in London. Her speech was reported in *Votes for Women*.

... At last they came. It is like describing a hospital scene – and much worse. The doctor and four wardresses came into my cell. I decided to save all my resistance for the actual feeding, and when they pointed to my bed on the floor, I lay down, and the doctor did not even feel my pulse. Two wardresses held my hands and one my head.

Much as I had heard about this thing, it was infinitely more horrible and more painful than I had expected. The doctor put the steel gag in somewhere on my gums and forced my mouth until it was yawning wide. As he proceeded to force into my mouth and down the throat a large rubber tube, I felt as though I was being killed – absolute suffocation is the feeling. You feel as though it would never stop. You cannot stop. You cannot breath and yet you choke. It irritates the throat, it irritates the mucous membrane as it goes down, every second seems an hour and you think they will never finish pushing it down.

After a while, the sensation is relieved, then the food is poured down, and then again you choke, and your whole body resists and writhes under the treatment; you are held down and the process goes on, and finally, when the vomiting becomes excessive, the tube is removed. I forgot what I was in there for, I forgot women, I forgot everything except my own sufferings, and I was completely overcome by them ...

Many, many women underwent the same treatment.

4

CONCILIATION FAILS

WHEN Lady Constance was released from Walton Gaol, the country was adjusting to the results of a general election which brought to an end the huge Liberal majority of 1906. The circumstances leading up to the election and the subsequent reactions of the parties to their changed fortunes had little to do with women's suffrage. They were, however, decisive in determining its fate.

The election of January 1910 was a stage in the struggle between the House of Commons and the House of Lords. In spite of their overwhelming majority in the former, the Liberal government had been thwarted in many of its proposed reforms by the Lords rejecting their Bills. They had had one outstanding success, the introduction of old age pensions, as this had been part of a Finance Bill which traditionally the Lords never opposed. Lloyd George decided to use this technique for a showdown, and in April 1909, he had introduced his Budget as a means of 'raising money to wage implacable war against poverty and squalidness'. All manner of tax increases were to be used to lay the foundations of what was to become the welfare state.

Throughout the summer, the parties fought with an asperity to which even Emmeline Pankhurst had hardly aspired. In the Commons, the Budget was fought over line by line in all-night sittings; in the country, packed meetings led to violence. It became the 'People's Budget' and the election cry was 'People versus Peers'.

When, in January, the votes were counted, the Liberals had 274 seats to the Conservatives' 273, and power lay with the Irish Nationalists with 82 and with the growing Labour Party's 41. The women could certainly claim that they had the support of a majority of the MPs, but as the great constitutional battle loomed, this support would be tempered by the MPs' allegiances to the objectives of their own parties.

The women's position was not a strong one. They controlled no parliamentary seats with which they could bargain in the negotiations that lay ahead. Nor did they have massive popular support, unlike that of the Labour Party through the trade unions. In fact, more anti-suffragist groups had recently been formed, and in 1909, a petition of 250,000 names against

The Lady Frances Balfour.

Elliott & Fry.

60. *Lady Frances Balfour came under acute pressure in 1910 and 1911. As President of the key London Society of the NUWSS, her efforts were directed towards maintaining Liberal backing for the Conciliation Bill. As sister-in-law of the Conservative Party leader, Arthur Balfour, she would have been identified with that party's embittered opposition to the reform of the House of Lords. Many other women faced the same dilemma. An indication of the way in which public opinion reserved judgement on the women's case is shown in the widely read* Lady's World *of November 1911. In an article about a leading women's club, The Lyceum, of which Lady Frances was also President, the editor finds it necessary to say: 'Now as nearly everyone knows, Lady Frances is one of the warmest and most consistent advocates of women's suffrage and her views have supporters at the Club; at the same time, there are numerous members who hold a totally different opinion and to whom the subject is entirely taboo.'*

" THE BATTLE OF STEPNEY ": Mr Winston Churchill in the Fire Zone

THE RIGHT DISHONOURABLE DOUBLE-FACE ASQUITH.

VOTES
FOR
WOMEN

Women's
Social and
Political
Union.

4,
Clement's
Inn,
London,
W.C.

Citizen Asq—th: " Down with privilege of birth—up with Democratic rule ! " | *Monseigneur Asq—th:* " The rights of government belong to the aristocrats by birth—men. No liberty or equality for women ! "

61.   Top: *A sense of crisis persisted throughout 1910 and 1911. Women's suffrage was not a political priority. Having survived two elections, the government was dependent on the support of minority parties but committed to ending the power of the House of Lords. On 4 January 1911, Churchill, while writing to Asquith to suggest creating 500 new peers to beat the Lords, rushed from his office to a house in Sidney Street in Stepney in the East End where the police supposedly had the anarchist terrorist 'Peter the Painter' under seige. Judging by the number of postcards that this episode provoked this activity was far more to the public's liking than the manoeuvring in Parliament.*

62.   Above: *This propaganda postcard from the WSPU is fair comment. Asquith's overriding objective and his ultimate achievement was the reform of the House of Lords, yet he showed no sympathy towards the women's movement until halfway through World War I.*

Published by The Women's Freedom League,
1, Robert Street, Adelphi, W.C.

63. *The WFL showed a talent for getting publicity without resorting to violence. Their boycott of the ten-yearly census on 2 April 1911 certainly aggravated Asquith as well as John Burns, the minister responsible. Burns, pictured here in his ceremonial dress as a Privy Councillor, was one of the early Labour MPs to join the Liberals, and was the first to reach ministerial rank. He was often mocked for having joined the establishment but, in this case, showed where his sympathies still lay by not prosecuting any of the boycotting women. Nevertheless they attracted wide press coverage, with stories of them avoiding registration by such subterfuges as camping overnight in Hyde Park. Punch made the more memorable comment: 'The ladies have taken leave of their census.'*

giving women the vote had been presented to Parliament. It was not only Lord Curzon – a former Viceroy of India – who opposed them in the Anti-Suffragist League, but women such as Mrs Humphry Ward and Lady Jersey. That women were seen to have a part to play either for or against suffrage was due to the intensive lobbying that the suffragists had built up over the years and the sense of urgency that the militants had brought. Valuable as this might be, it would have to compete with other claims for parliamentary reform – for constitutional rights which, Liberals would argue, went as far back as Magna Carta; for Irish Home Rule which nationalists had sought for centuries; and for universal adult suffrage which the Labour Party espoused as the basis of true democracy.

The very tightness of the election result emphasised these attitudes. The Liberals would still govern – but only with the support of the Irish Nationalists. Having gained this support with a promise to reform the powers of the House of Lords and thus open the way to Irish Home Rule, the controversial Budget was finally passed in April – one year late. Only a few days later, Edward VII died and constitutional processes were again in turmoil.

The Conciliation Bill

In an attempt to ease tension, an all-party committee to consider a solution to the question of women's suffrage was set up. Lord Lytton, Lady Constance's brother, became its chairman, and she and others were active behind the scenes. The militants called a truce with the government while the Conciliation Committee, as it came to be called, carried out its work.

As if to emphasise their strength of purpose in the absence of militancy, the women filled the early summer months with a series of rallies, processions and meetings. Once again the gorgeous banners spread above the marching ranks: here was 'General' Drummond leading a parade on horseback to the cheers of the crowd; and in the Albert Hall, vast throngs hailed their leaders and generously gave donations. Civic dignitaries backed their cause, and Asquith found time to meet the constitutional societies.

In June, the Conciliation Committee produced a draft Bill. It proposed giving the vote to women having property rights and it was passed with a majority of 110. It was a Pyrrhic victory. To gain conservative support, the proposals were based on the privilege of property and it lost the backing of many natural radicals among the Liberals including Lloyd George and Churchill. Churchill had become Home Secretary and had already introduced

militants. On 'Black Friday' – 18 November 1909 – violence spontaneously erupted, and for six hours, women struggled with police in Parliament Square. Prison conditions may have improved, but now the police appeared not to be making arrests but dealing with the women as if they were rowdies in a football crowd.

The December election produced an almost identical result to that of January, with the government's survival still depending on the smaller parties. Postcards played a minor but interesting part. In Hornsey, in London, a postcard opinion poll was taken to assess support for female suffrage: 22,350 reply-paid postcards were dispatched; there were 7,500 replies, but only 2,200 supported votes for

64. *The coronation of George V enabled all of the suffrage organisations to demonstrate their unity peaceably while the Conciliation Bill was going through the House of Commons. Their procession was so large that it stretched along the Embankment from Westminster to Blackfriars and spilled into the adjoining side streets. This postcard shows it winding its way to Hyde Park past some of the temporary stands erected for the coronation procession itself. The contingent in the front carries the banner of the Actresses' Franchise League.*

65. *The intricacies of the Conciliation Bills were too complex for postcards. The NUWSS did its best to publicise the issues. This announcement is from their weekly paper* The Common Cause *of 27 July 1911 and was also printed in leaflet form for wider distribution. Having won the majority of 167 for the second reading of the Conciliation Bill in May, it shows just how firm the NUWSS had to be in getting ministers to allow sufficient parliamentary time for the next stage. Unfortunately, when that time came in March of the following year, the attitudes of many MPs had changed and the Bill was lost by 14 votes.*

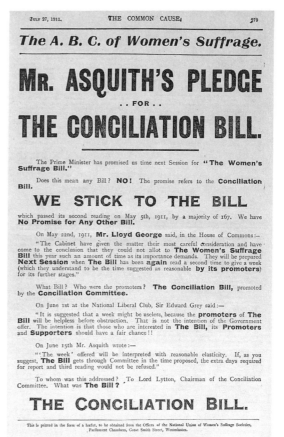

measures to improve the lot of suffragettes in prison by allowing them to keep their own clothes, and have regular exercise – 'first division' treatment. But when speaking against the Conciliation Bill, he condemned it as undemocratic and the Bill was referred back to committee.

By November the women's frustrations overflowed. Asquith now had to pay his debt to the Irish Nationalists to reform the House of Lords, and for that, he needed the approval of another general election. He announced it in November, and although he satisfied the constitutionalist societies by promising that, if returned to power, time would be given for a Suffrage Bill, this move infuriated the

This is "THE HOUSE" that man built,
And these are the Suffragettes of note
Determined to fight for their right to vote;
For they mean to be, each one an M. P.
And they'll keep their vow some fine day you'll see,
For the Suffragette is determined to get
Into "THE HOUSE" that man built.

This is "THE HOUSE" that man built,
And these are a few of the Ladies of Fame
Anxious to write M. P. after their name,
With each sex on a par, why put up the bar?
For M. P. means either Mama or Papa,
Quoth the sweet Suffragette we're entitled to get
Into "THE HOUSE" that man built.

This is "THE HOUSE" that man built,
And this is the Minister weary and worn
Who treated the Suffragette with scorn,
Who wanted a Vote, and (a saying to quote),
Dared him to tread on the tail of the coat
Of the bold Suffragette determined to get.
Into "THE HOUSE" that man built.

THIS IS
"THE HOUSE"
THAT MAN BUILT,

AND this is the
Suffragette lady
of note
Who once used
A BRICK
for recording her vote,
Who one fine day went
With the fullest intent;
To show the Prime Minister
business was meant,
But the bold Suffragette
THRO' THE WINDOW
cant get;
Into THE HOUSE
that man built.

THIS IS "THE HOUSE" THAT MAN BUILT

ER RULES & AND REGULATIONS

AND this is the poor little Suffragette Who tried, Oh so hard, in this HOUSE to get: Tho' it wasn't a crime Still with patience sublime She spends the best part of her life doing time; OH FIE! Suffragette Be contented to get In your OWN little house, that man built.

FROM PRISON TO CITIZENSHIP

This is "THE HOUSE" that man built, And this is the Flag of the Woman's Franchise, Which is making our Ministers open their eyes: Fighting with grit, to the front bit by bit; Determined in Parliament one day to sit, The bold Suffragette who is sure to get yet Into "THE HOUSE" that man built.

This is "THE HOUSE" that man built But oh what a wonderful change inside The women as well as the men preside They both hold the reins & no one complains For the men now admit that the ladies have brains And are every bit quite as fitted to sit As themselves, in this House that man built.

66-72. *The spirit of conciliation no doubt inspired these cards. They are from two sets and show the suffragettes not as Victorian harridans or domineering academics but as smartly dressed, capable women. A number of them depict specific incidents of the campaign, but rather than ridiculing the women, they sometimes offer a little encouragement or hope. In one example, the banner 'From Prison to Citizenship' is the one under which almost 1,000 ex-prisoners marched in the Coronation procession of 1911, and the legend reads: 'the bold suffragette . . . is sure to get yet into "The House" that man built.' Similarly, the suffragette with the brick could represent Mrs Pankhurst's attack on the windows of No. 10 Downing Street on 1 March 1912. Most encouraging of all is the final picture showing men and women working amicably in the House of Commons itself.*

women. It was another indication that, despite all the women's activity and publicity, the movement still lacked grassroots support.

The election breathed new life into the Conciliation Bill. A revised version meeting Churchill's criticisms came before the House for a second reading in May and, with the parties preoccupied with the coming showdown with the Lords, received a majority of 167 in favour. Summer days were here again. The spirit of

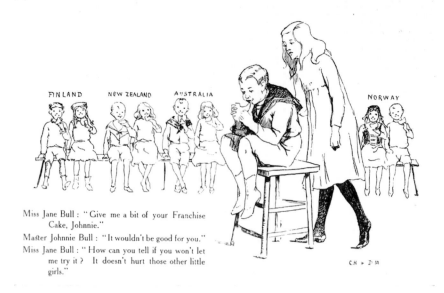

FINLAND   NEW ZEALAND   AUSTRALIA   NORWAY

Miss Jane Bull : "Give me a bit of your Franchise Cake, Johnnie."

Master Johnnie Bull : "It wouldn't be good for you."

Miss Jane Bull : "How can you tell if you won't let me try it ? It doesn't hurt those other little girls."

C.H ► J·M

73. Top: *Mrs Pankhurst's visit to the United States in 1911 underlined the international nature of women's suffrage. This postcard got the message across in a way that even children could understand. Women achieved the vote in New Zealand in 1893, in Australia in 1902, in Finland in 1905 and in Norway in 1907. The card might also have referred to Wyoming (1869), Colorado (1893), and Idaho and Utah (1896). Washington State and California followed in, respectively, 1910 and 1911 in time for Mrs Pankhurst's arrival.*

74. Above: *Mrs Pankhurst's fame had already reached the Americans. Postcards published there in 1909 used the word 'suffragette' and did her the honour of being printed in the colours of the WSPU.*

truce returned, and on 17 June, ten days before the coronation of George V, the combined women's organisations presented their most lavish procession. As they marched once more to Hyde Park, they must have felt that they had weathered the storm and that they now had only to get their ship into port. Emmeline Pankhurst even left the country for a lecture tour of the United States.

Disaffection

Asquith brought the dread chill of winter when he announced in November that the government intended to introduce legislation for adult male suffrage; this would invalidate the Conciliation Bill as it was based on the existing laws of franchise. Recognising the position of the Conciliation Bill, he proposed that if the House of Commons wished, an amendment could include women's suffrage.

The women's patience broke. They were not interested in manoeuvring to hold the Labour Party in check, or in widening the franchise to counteract a Conservative revival. They just wanted to vote. Protests and violence broke out immediately; large numbers of arrests were made. Lloyd George announced that he was ready to lead the fight in the Commons to secure the amendment for women's suffrage, but he was branded a turncoat. Extremists began to call for a war of the sexes, and long-standing suffragists drew back in alarm.

Emmeline Pankhurst arrived back from the United States in January. She had already condemned the government and now urged more militant action. Later that month, when Lloyd George was addressing the NUWSS in the Albert Hall, the WSPU constantly interrupted and almost broke up the meeting. As the rift with the government widened, the women began to lose touch with each other. Then on 1 March, women took hammers and stones and broke shop windows from Picadilly Circus, up Regent Street and along most of Oxford Street, and in other parts of the West End; Mrs Pankhurst and two colleagues went to No. 10 Downing Street and threw stones at Asquith's windows. Violence against property had begun.

The escalation of violent protest was the militants' only weapon. The tactics they had used to gain publicity for their cause and the pressures on governments that they had learned from Parnell, were now the only methods they could employ once negotiations broke down. As the weeks went by, they brought less and less success. The break with the suffragists – so carefully concealed in the past – now visibly widened. The power of the anti-suffragists, previously scorned, now answered them speech for speech, petition for petition. And recovering from its initial surprise, the government was ready to act.

On 5 March, only four days after the mass window-breaking, the government arrested the leaders of the WSPU on charges of conspiracy. Christabel had heard about the warrant for her arrest before the police found her and had fled to Paris in the first of many cloak-and-dagger exploits. Emmeline Pankhurst and the Pethick Lawrences were sent for

75. *Christabel Pankhurst grew in stature to become, like her mother, a national figure. A tough debater, she could hold audiences with the skill of an actress. The crowds loved it and called her 'Chrissy'. She is the 'Miss Hissy' of this cartoon. Although in many ways derogatory, this postcard would have publicised the Union's name and helped people to understand the significance of gender.*

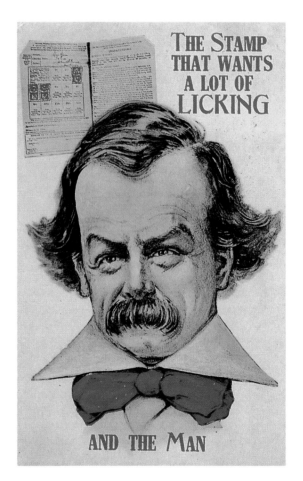

THE STAMP
THAT WANTS
A LOT OF
LICKING

AND THE MAN

STICKING TO IT !

IT'S ON THE TIP
OF MY TONGUE!

FORCIBLE
FEEDING

LICK!

76-78. *One of Lloyd George's great achievements was the introduction of National Insurance following the victory over the Lords with his 'People's Budget' – the first step towards a welfare state. The scheme was financed – as it still is – by contributions from the government, employers and employees. It entailed sticking contribution stamps on to the insurance card, and the act of licking them gave rise to dozens of postcard jokes. Most were complimentary to Lloyd George, but because many women felt that he had betrayed them by not giving wholehearted support to the Conciliation Bills, some put their tongues out at him and others compared the system unfavourably to forcible feeding.*

trial at the Old Bailey. The trial did not have the effect of the earlier Bow Street confrontation. The defendants pleaded with skill and conviction, but the prosecution had ample evidence to prove its case. They each received sentences of nine months' imprisonment.

It was not the trial but its aftermath that had the greater impact. Christabel, running the WSPU from Paris with Annie Kenney as the nominal head making weekly trips across the Channel, took an increasingly hard line. The Pethick Lawrences on their release from prison, where they had undergone the torments of forcible feeding, tried to rethink a strategy.

WHEN WOMAN RULES

"Fed-up."

CHURCH SOCIALIST SERIES.   GEORGE LANSBURY, M.P., L.C.C.   PHOTO BY H. HARRISON

79. Top: *Directly the WSPU broke its truce with the government, the latter reintroduced forcible feeding. Such callous treatment of women by those in authority was only matched by the insensitivity of the public which regarded it as a subject for fun.*

80. Above: *George Lansbury, one of the Labour Party's idealists, felt so deeply committed to women's rights and so outraged at their 'torture' in prison that he resigned the seat he had won at Bromley & Bow in December 1910 in order to seek re-election on the issue of women's suffrage. He received no backing from the Labour Party and even sympathisers such as Philip Snowden felt that the militants had forfeited his support. On 26 November 1912, Lansbury lost this election by 731 votes. He went on to become leader of the Labour Party between 1931 and 1935.*

Circumstances were changing and they could not clearly see a way ahead. To Emmeline and Christabel Pankhurst, there was still only one way, so that, while continuing to publish *Votes for Women*, the Pethick Lawrences withdrew from the WSPU. Their departure had a far more grievous effect than that of Charlotte Despard, whose reasons for splitting with the Pankhursts may well have been similar to the Pethick Lawrences'. It left the WSPU without their administrative and political skills, and importantly, it allowed others to see the limitations of militancy.

MPs had already seen those limits. On 28 March 1912, a third Conciliation Bill, similar to its predecessor, came before the House. It was defeated by 14 votes, compared to the earlier majority of 167 in favour. The MPs had no incentive to support the Bill; the Irish Nationalists' sole concern was to enable Asquith to survive as Prime Minister; many Labour and Liberal MPs preferred fighting for universal adult suffrage; some others used the opportunity to oppose militant methods; and perhaps others were just bored.

Disarray

With the constitutional societies estranged as well as the House of Commons, and the Pankhursts becoming ever more extremist, the movement lacked a sense of direction. Individual acts of violence occurred haphazardly. Asquith and Lloyd George suffered personal attacks. Mary Leigh, the first woman to have been subjected to forcible feeding back in 1909, threw a hatchet at Asquith in Dublin and then, with two others, set fire to the Theatre Royal. The WSPU's policy, as far as it now had one, was directed against property. It had begun with the breaking of the shop windows when Emmeline Pankhurst had declared that damage to property would make her opponents think. It also had the advantage of securing quick arrests and thus releasing the women from the tougher handling now being meted out by the police. By 1912, these tactics had reached the point where buildings were regularly being burned down.

There was a hiatus in political relationships. Paradoxically the Conservative MPs now seemed to offer the women more reliable, if more limited, backing. The Conciliation Bills were far more to their liking than the more sweeping proposals of the Liberals and Labour. Emmeline and Christabel, who had come to enjoy their contacts in London's fashionable houses, felt drawn towards them, but Sylvia Pankhurst, who valued her personal ties with such Labour leaders as Keir Hardie and George Lansbury, stayed faithful to her work in the East End. Like Charlotte Despard and the Pethick Lawrences, she came to reject her mother's and sister's policies, and the WSPU bore another loss. Even Millicent Fawcett, a life-long Liberal, became so disenchanted by the government's ambivalence that she cast around for alternative political allies. Finally, the NUWSS gave support to selected Labour candidates.

The government itself, trembling on the tightrope held by the Irish Nationalists, was also in some contusion. In April 1912, Asquith had introduced a Home Rule Bill which was being fought as bitterly as had been the 'People's Budget'. Worse still, the Unionists were threatening action outside Parliament, and the risk of civil war was never far away.

This was of little concern to women but when, in January 1913, the government's own Franchise Bill was stopped in its tracks, they could hardly believe what they heard. The Speaker of the House ruled that the amendment to add women's suffrage – with which Lloyd George had identified himself – would so alter the nature of the Bill that it would require complete redrafting. By that one decision, the whole of the government's plans for franchise reform had to be reworked. The Prime Minister was as surprised as the women, but not so deeply hurt. For them, there was now no clear way ahead. There would be more Private Members' Bills – and there were – but like the others they came to nothing.

Emmeline Pankhurst now worked with a blind resolution. She and her adherents were caught in a conflict which carried them from one increasingly desperate outrage to another. They broke windows indiscriminately, burned the tea rooms at Kew and vandalised public places. In February, showing a more considered sense of purpose, they blew up a house being built for Lloyd George at Walton Heath. This could not be ignored, and Mrs Pankhurst stepped forward to take the blame. Her trial did nothing to stop the outrages, and she was sentenced to three years' imprisonment.

It was now the government's turn to raise the stakes. Forcible feeding did not prevent the health of prisoners on hunger strike from quickly deteriorating, and they were often released long before the completion of their sentences. Against cries from the diehards that militant women should be left to starve, be birched and deported, the new Home Secretary,

DON'T BE SURPRISED IF IT'S YOUR WIFE WHO DOCTORS THE GREENS!

81. & 82. *By 1913, political protest had degenerated into outrages against property. The top postcard shows a photograph of Levetleigh, St Leonards after it had been burned down by the suffragettes on 15 April 1913. They claimed that no one was ever in the buildings they attacked and that no one was ever hurt. Insurance companies faced enormous claims. Earlier in the year the greens of a number of golf courses near Birmingham were ruined by acid spread in the name of women's suffrage. The North British Rubber Co. Ltd used these incidents in postcards advertising the durability of their golf balls.*

Reginald McKenna, was ready to ask for new powers. His Prisoners' (Temporary Discharge for Ill Health) Bill allowed prisoners to be released on medical grounds and, when once again fit, rearrested to complete their sentences.

Dubbed the 'Cat and Mouse Act' it enabled the police to keep released prisoners under continual surveillance and, at any sign of trouble, to rearrest them. The suffragettes soon learned how to outwit them with disguises and false trails, or with groups of women shielding the prisoner from the police and standing in their way while an escape was made. All this was good for morale and gained a little publicity, but it could hardly work with a woman as notorious as Emmeline Pankhurst. Between April 1913 and July 1914, invariably weak from numerous hunger strikes and often at the point of death, she was moved in and out of prison nineteen times.

83. *Emily Davison's funeral on 14 June 1913 became a memorial parade for the WSPU. Thousands of women in black or in the Union's colours escorted her body from Victoria Station to King's Cross on its way to a family burial in Northumberland. Mrs Pankhurst was to have ridden behind the hearse, but as she left to go there, she was immediately arrested under the provisions of the 'Cat and Mouse Act'. Instead, her empty carriage followed the coffin.*

Another woman who courted death was Emily Wilding Davison. She was a person of talent. A first-class honours degree in English from Oxford was accompanied by a vivid imagination. She was one of the first to have spoken of 'dying for the cause'. Once, in prison, she had thrown herself from a high walkway on to the netting which had been placed there to prevent suicides. In June, at Epsom races, she threw herself under the hooves of the King's horse in the Derby and died in hospital. Of all the acts perpetrated by the suffragettes, her death must have gained them more publicity than any other.

So the violence went on: the burning of houses, sports pavilions, seaside piers, churches; arguing and fighting in court rooms; the interruption of State occasions; and constant skirmishing with police. The only thing that the militants respected seemed to be human life.

One incident has long been remembered and its effects can still be seen. On 10 March 1914, Mary Richardson slashed Velázquez's painting of a female nude, known as the *Rokeby Venus*, in the National Gallery. She said: 'I have tried to destroy the picture of the most beautiful woman in mythological history as a protest against the government for destroying Mrs Pankhurst who is the most beautiful character in modern history.'

5

WOMEN AND WORLD WAR I

MILITANCY of another type led to Germany's unprovoked invasion of Belgium in August 1914, and put British affairs in a different perspective. Women realised this as quickly as the government. At the very outset of the war, both Millicent Fawcett for the NUWSS and Emmeline Pankhurst for the WSPU issued statements urging women to back the government. Suffragette prisoners were released early and they started volunteering for the Red Cross, the relief committees and similar organisations. By the end of the month, they were helping to cope with the arrival of a quarter of a million Belgian refugees.

These were not direct actions by the suffrage movement itself, but they were a measure of the change in attitudes which the women's movement as a whole had brought about over the thirty years that had passed since the disappointment of Gladstone's Reform Act. Women – whose mothers would have winced at attending a public meeting and fainted at the thought of a young woman going about unchaperoned – were now ready and eager to take on another role. Many had already had experience of going out to work and of knowing the satisfaction and sense of freedom that earning money can bring. Most were better educated than their mothers, and all had confidence in themselves. This had been the achievement of the suffrage movement. It may not yet have won women the vote, but it had enabled them to believe in themselves. The campaign for votes – and the sheer détermination of the militants – had enabled a new generation of women to aspire to Mary Wollstonecraft's objective, 'to attain a character as a human being'.

UNITED!

84. *This card is typical of the patriotic fervour of 1914 and groups the minority factions in British politics around the Union Jack. But Irish Nationalists and Pro-Ulster Unionists were to fight a civil war in Ireland, and pacifists in the Labour Party such as Ramsay MacDonald and George Lansbury were to withdraw from public life for the duration. Only the women's movement gave unstinting support.*

Women and war work

In the first chaotic months of the war, more women volunteered for work than the authorities knew how to employ. Dr Louisa Garrett Anderson (daughter of the trail blazer Elizabeth) and Dr Flora Murray could not follow normal recruitment paths for military medical service, so they set up their own hospital in France. Similarly the War Office did not take up Dr Elsie Inglis's offer to organise and staff complete medical units. Undeterred she worked through the Scottish NUWSS, of which she was secretary, and with their help, she set up the Scottish Women's Hospitals which sent hospital units to the fronts overseas.

Such individual efforts as these were later incorporated into the official system, within which the Voluntary Aid Detachments began rapidly expanding. The VADs had developed from the experience of the Boer War and drew on voluntary labour for stretcher bearers and medical attendants. So great was the response – 23,000 men and 47,000 women volunteered – that the training facilities were overwhelmed. It was not until October that the first VAD unit left for France, but thereafter their activities expanded into most sectors of the fighting, with women taking on all manner of work as cooks, orderlies, telephonists and bookkeepers. Later some became ambulance drivers, their numbers growing from a mere dozen in 1915 to several hundred by the end of the war.

However, the major problem in 1914 was the change brought about by the war-time economy: the country needed armaments and food. Hundreds of thousands of men volunteered for the army, yet although willing to work and with over 200,000 losing jobs in the declining luxury trades, women remained unemployed. In the spring of 1915, the government introduced a registration scheme for national service to ascertain the nation's capacity. Although 87,000 women registered, only 2,332 were found work. Much of the difficulty was due to the fact that the trade unions in the engineering industry resisted 'dilution' of men's jobs, fearing, as always, that semi-skilled women would do the work for lower pay. Generalized prejudice against women also remained strong, with farmers asking for schoolboys to help them.

In May 1915, the government was re-formed as a coalition of all parties, and Lloyd George as Minister of Munitions was given the job of reorganising industry. The women backed him. On 17 July, the suffrage societies mounted a parade through London of some 30,000 women carrying banners saying 'We demand the right to serve.' It recalled the pre-war processions, but this time the government and the press were on their side.

The development of an efficient munitions industry was one of the major achievements of the war. Lloyd George hammered out agreements with the engineering trade unions, fixing equal pay for piecework only against a guarantee of maintaining wage rates and a return to previous practice at the end of the war. New training centres for women were set up along with huge government-financed production facilities. By the end of the war, 750,000 women worked in the munitions industry.

As more men enlisted, so more jobs opened up for women. The government itself recruited 162,000 as clerical workers, partly as substitutes for men and partly for the new war-time ministries. The London County Council went further by training women as plumbers, carpenters and electricians to combat the shortage of tradesmen. A leading bank claimed that it had filled the jobs of 1,800 men with 1,300 women and was completely satisfied with the results – but made no mention of the costs it must have saved.

As the war went on, it appeared that there were few things that women could not do. They became fire fighters, chimney sweeps, house painters, gas workers, blacksmiths, bakers – almost any job that they were given a chance to tackle – so that only such hidebound occupations as the judiciary and stockbroking seemed closed to them. Postcards welcomed them, not as caricatures or militants, but for what they were: hard-working people.

Nursing, of course, was one employment area in which they were pre-eminent. Florence Nightingale had long since established their professional capability. At the outbreak of war, the Royal Army Medical Corps could barely meet the requirements of the new British Expeditionary Force in France, and the Queen Alexandra Imperial Military Nursing Service comprised only 463 nurses. By the end of the war, this number had grown to 7,835 with an additional 4,958 untrained staff. The British Red Cross and St John Ambulance experienced even greater growth, from 2,354 to over 120,000, many of whom were volunteers.

The trained nurse was an intrinsic part of the medical service. Her work went far beyond the general concept of caring for the wounded. She assisted with surgical work, helped develop treatments for the new circumstances of war – gas, shell shock, trench foot – and initiated methods of rehabilitation. As the war continued, the control of diseases and infections with inoculations and vaccines became more important, especially in the Middle East where many nurses worked to control the spread of malaria and other tropical diseases. Later, as war took its toll, they entered new areas such as orthopaedics and psychotherapy.

The nurses were assisted by large numbers of partially trained or untrained women workers. The VADs had shown the way. Soon women took on those thousands of essential but routine jobs which receive little public acclaim. Female cleaners, orderlies, cooks, hairdressers, dispensers and dental assistants swelled the ranks of the medical services. Many served in France and, later, in other theatres of war. Often they were joined by women from Commonwealth countries – Australia, Canada and South Africa – supporting Britain in the war.

All over the country, hundreds of hospitals were

FUSE FACTORY, WOOLWICH ARSENAL.

MUNITION WORKER'S NOV 1916

85. Top: *Woolwich Arsenal was one of the major munition factories. Handling dangerous explosives, women made shells, bullets and cartridges. Very often they would work on automatic or semi-automatic processes but soon showed an aptitude for skilled jobs. A report to the British Association in 1915 stated that, with the exception of the very heaviest tools, women could operate as efficiently as men. They particularly excelled in making fuses – of which this postcard is a photographic record – and in the delicate manufacture of aeroplane wings.*

86. Above: *The women munition workers, always very patriotic, also enjoyed the companionship that they found in the workplace as well as the opportunity to earn wages. In many factories, 'uniforms' were worn as a safety precaution: hats prevented hair becoming entangled in machines, and for the first time, women began to wear trousers since they were safer than long skirts. Facilities for lodging and eating were often poor, but the government set up a Welfare and Health Department which trained staff for welfare work.*

I suppose a woman can fill up forms
as well as a man?

89. & 90. Right: *The general public became most aware of working women by their employment in transport services where they replaced men in large numbers. The London underground system used them as lift operators, ticket collectors and gate women. They became conductors of both trams and buses in spite of early threats by men in some provincial depots to close the service down. The London General Omnibus Co. alone employed 2,100 women. Women conductors and underground staff were commended for their calmness and the assistance they gave passengers during air raids on London.*

91. Bottom right: *Even the farmers came round to using women. In 1915, MPs had joked about 'pretty milkmaids'; by 1916, they were a reality. Women's War Agricultural Committees had sprung up like newly sewn seed and, by 1917, were incorporated into a Women's Land Army. Thirty thousand more women – all were volunteers – received special training, and a magazine,* The Landswoman, *became a regular source of information. The system was so successful that it continued into 1919.*

87. *This postcard is far from fair. When women registered for war work in 1915, they were not squeezing men out of jobs. The card reveals all the pre-war prejudices about women which later cards were to lose. At least it still displayed the colours of the WSPU.*

92. Bottom far right: *The appearance of women police raised quite a few eyebrows. This really was an about-turn from the pre-war days when militants and police fought pitched battles in Parliament Square. Dorothy Pethick, Emmeline's sister, made one of the most dramatic changes. She had accompanied Lady Constance on her stone-throwing foray to Newcastle, but in 1914 she was a policewoman. The official name of the female police was the Women's Auxiliary Service, and they operated particularly in areas with munitions factories as well as being part of the more rigorous control at ports and stations.*

88. Left: *By 1916, women workers were not only generally accepted but praised for their ability and public spirit. This card with the 'lady tram conductor', the 'post lady' and the 'lady window cleaners' is in sharp contrast to those that showed the fearsome umbrella-brandishing women of Edwardian days. Uniforms denoted an acceptable militancy, trousers a permissable symbol of equality with men.*

Pay your Fare and you can Ride
There's room on top and room
inside.

Prices are rather high this year,
Even our Milkman's a "little dear."

A FAIR COP.

Ladies Committee, Soldiers & Sailors Sewing Party 1914.

93. & **94.** *Voluntary work was no less important than paid employment. All over the country, thousands of women were engaged in some form of war work: they ran canteens at railway stations; sent parcels to men at the front; organised War Savings campaigns; helped the Soldiers' and Sailors' Families Association; and generally took on anything that had to be done. As the photographic postcard (top) shows, ladies committees for sewing clothes for soldiers and sailors were active as early as 1914. They no doubt were the origin of the children's tongue twister 'Sister Susie's sewing shirts for soldiers.' The bottom card shows a group at Reading raising money for the wounded on one of the numerous flag days.*

THE GIRLS RECKON THEY CAN DO ANYTHING WITHOUT US MEN NOW-A-DAYS

BUT CAN THEY?

"We can't bear arms, but we can bear armies!"

95. & 96. *While recognising women's increasing activities, World War I postcards also had the temerity to raise the question of childbirth and motherhood. The subject had hardly been mentioned in all the pre-war rhetoric. It has still not been satisfactorily resolved. And after the war, many women felt alienated by the way in which their mothers had allowed sons and brothers to be sent off to be killed.*

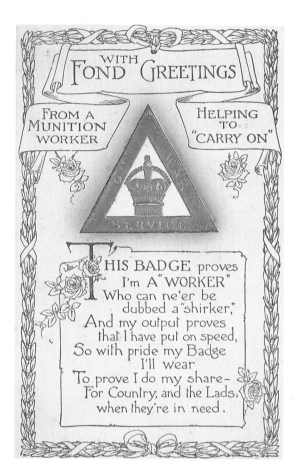

WITH FOND GREETINGS

FROM A MUNITION WORKER

HELPING TO "CARRY ON"

THIS BADGE proves
I'm A "WORKER"
Who can ne'er be
   dubbed a "shirker,"
And my output proves
   that I have put on speed,
So with pride my Badge
   I'll wear
To prove I do my share—
For Country, and the Lads,
   when they're in need.

EVERY PICTURE TELLS A STORY.

97. Above left: *Government recognition of working women's contribution to the war effort came in the form of a triangular badge inscribed 'On War Service'. A number of photographic postcards of women proudly wearing the small triangle pinned to their chests can be found.*

98. Above right: *'War Service' could take many forms. There is pathos in the message written on the back of this card:*
    My Dear Wife,
    Keep your head up Love. Hope you got my Address all right. It is No 9 Winifred Street Blackpool. Am still in Good Health. Have just been Enocklated. Best of Love to you All at Home. Your Loving Husband, George.'

99. Left: *No one questioned women's capabilities as nurses — on the contrary, the publishers of postcards revered them. Idealised images combined concepts of beauty, love and motherly care with the professionalism of a uniform. When stories circulated of the angel at the battle of Mons, some even assumed heavenly attributes.*

100. *Few believed that women could be ambulance drivers, particularly in a war zone. However, the RAMC soon found that it was ill equipped to move wounded men from the battlefield to military hospitals, and voluntary groups began to provide ambulances, many of which had teams of workers similar to those shown in this picture. Some of them are wearing VAD hats and armbands; the water bottles they carry were as much for the wounded as for themselves. The teams worked in France throughout the war and did all the mechanical maintenance on their vehicles. They often displayed great courage working under fire, and a number of women won military medals.*

101. *This is the 'Old Cook' at the Queen Alexandra Military Hospital. The quality of food seems to have varied. One worker wrote:*
Then I went to do work at an officers' hospital. Four of us slept in an attic and we had to get up at six. It was hard work but quite fun because I liked the people. There were no food restrictions there, everything was lavish.

Another worker had quite a different experience:
When fish was dreadfully dear and there was a shortage of potatoes, we put some rice in the fish cakes, and a note came down on one tray addressed to 'Madame the Cook'. 'Fish rissoles should be made of fish' was the message. I sent a note in return: 'Sir, perhaps you have not observed that we are at war and there is a food shortage.' The poor man had had a leg off and was wounded in the head so if anyone knew what war was he did. I found this out afterwards but in answer to my note all he said was: 'Dear me, is that so?'

102. & **103.** *The execution of Nurse Cavell on 12 October 1915, provoked outrage in Britain comparable to that felt when German submarines had sunk the* Lusitania *the previous May. She had been accused of helping British soldiers to escape and had been sentenced to death. At the place of execution, she had fainted and the firing squad had hesitated to shoot. The officer in charge took out his revolver and shot her in the head. The picture of this incident appears on a French card and the cartoon is one of a famous series by Tito Corbella deriding 'German culture'.*

Nurse Cavell was commemorated after the war by statues in London (almost opposite St Martin-in-the-Fields), at her home city of Norwich, and at the place of execution itself. There were many postcards of her. Her death may have marked the turning point when the country came to accept that women should no longer be excluded from national affairs.

opened up to care for the wounded. The letters of the women staff tell their own story:

When I was VAD-ing I began work in a small country hospital. I was nineteen, very carefully brought up and severely chaperoned. So you may imagine that the war seemed to open a new world to me. I passed suddenly from being the kind of girl I was to being a little person who spent her time in a hospital freeing from lice the uniforms of the soldiers who were brought in!

and;

I began my VAD work about a year after the outbreak of war. Naturally I supposed that, with so many young and strong volunteers, elderly women would not be required . . . There was a deep sense of unrest and excitement that had a particularly unsettling effect on the younger women of the nation and this caused certain difficulties. . . It was owing to this that a certain number of elderly VADs were recruited, especially for night duty in our town hospital.

Amidst the turmoil of war, women were not only playing a full part – they were discovering themselves.

The death of one nurse, Edith Cavell, touched the hearts of the whole nation. Daughter of a Norfolk vicar, she had studied medicine in Belgium and Germany and, in 1900, had become superintendent of the Highgate Infirmary in London. Returning to Brussels as matron of the Ecole Belge d'Infirmiers Diplomées, she decided to remain there when the war broke out, caring for the sick and wounded of all nations. On 5 August 1915, she was charged with helping British soldiers to escape and was sentenced to death. The callous nature of her execution on 12 October as well as the sentence made the general public realise the sacrifice which so many women were making. Asquith, who for so many years had doubted the capabilities of women, was moved to say: 'There are thousands of such women, but a year ago we did not know it.'

Perhaps politicians knew it now, but what would they do about it?

Suffrage reform

For the first two years of the war, nobody mentioned women's suffrage. Not Emmeline Pankhurst or Millicent Fawcett, both of whom actively supported the government in its war effort. Nor did Asquith and Lloyd George, who had quite enough on their hands to deal with; nor the Labour Party, wrestling with its own traumas over pacifism; nor the general public for whom Kaiser Bill had replaced the suffragette as a topic for cartoons or jokes in the pub. Neither, yet, did the women themselves, immersed as they were in war work and knowing perhaps that one day their time would come. Even Lord Curzon and Mrs Humphry Ward hid behind a frosty silence as they saw their anti-suffrage followers melt away.

In the summer of 1916, Millicent Fawcett allowed herself a murmur. The NUWSS had remained in existence. It had lost some pacifist and left-wing members, but its insistence on remaining free from political questions other than women's suffrage had held the societies together. The NUWSS had watched and waited, and when a suggestion was made that a new voting register based on war service should be drawn up, they were ready to comment.

All agreed on the need for a new register. The addresses shown on the existing register no longer applied to 80 per cent of male electors and there was no provision for those doing war service. The

NUWSS, while insisting that it did not wish to dissipate the government's energies by a controversial argument, stated that it would not stand by and allow voting rights to be extended to hundreds of thousands of serving men while nothing was done for serving women.

For the first time, Asquith agreed. He asked Parliament for its view and the MPs said that the government should decide. Once again, 'Votes for Women' became a subject for open debate, and this time it had clear support from the public, politicians and the press. Postcards, however, do not appear to have made any mention of it, perhaps because it was now something that was no longer really in dispute. Besides, postcard publishers preferred pictures of what women were actively doing, not comments on more manoeuvring among the politicians.

In August 1916, Asquith declared his own support, not simply because of what women were doing in the war but – and here he must have been thinking of the munitions workers – for the part they would be entitled to play in the process of industrial reconstruction afterwards. An all-party conference, chaired by the Speaker of the House of Commons, was set up to draft proposals for the revision of the franchise.

When the proposals were ready in January 1917,

Lloyd George had become Prime Minister, the first to be an open advocate of women's suffrage. There were few men in his government – and perhaps not many more in the country – who would have denied women the vote. The normal processes of consultations followed. But, despite the obvious support for female suffrage, women's voting rights were to be restricted to householders and those aged over thirty-five. The suffrage societies, and especially the Labour Party supporters who knew that the industrial workers were mainly younger women, agonised over the restrictions, but all finally agreed that, if a reduction to the age of thirty could be conceded, they would accept the proposals. To drive home their point, they held a massive demonstration – one composed not of the pre-war suffrage societies but of the women war workers.

It remained for Millicent Fawcett, remembering the fate of the Reform Bill in 1913, to ensure that the clauses concerning women's suffrage were part of the whole Bill and not merely an amendment. Lloyd George accepted this. On 19 June 1917, the clause granting the vote to women over thirty was passed by a majority of 385 to 55, and only the final legislative hurdles of parliamentary procedures were left to be cleared.

Women in military service

While parliamentarians took these momentous steps, women marched forward in military uniforms. In March 1917, the Women's Auxiliary Army Corps – the WAAC – was created. It grew from the Women's Legion which had been providing the army with cooks and drivers, and from the employment of civilians in military activities. By the end of 1916, it had become apparent that women could replace men in a

104. & **105.**   *The creation of female military units seemed to confuse postcard publishers, who appeared to be as unsure of their purpose as they were of their uniforms. The French actually made an official enquiry asking who and what they were, and the French postcard, with Gallic logic, put it all down to the suffragettes. Cartoonists found it easy to make jokes about WAACs, but Wrens and WRAFs seemed impregnable.*

I'm not greedy- but I like a fair W.A.A.C

THE CITADEL
BAGHDAD

With Best Wishes
for Xmas and
the New Year

106. *17,000 WAACs served overseas, some with the 'forgotten army' in the Middle East. Not everybody forgot them as this card shows. The Women of Bombay published this one as part of a fund-raising series.*

range of non-combatant duties and that there was no reason why they should not serve overseas. With more and more men being needed at the front, it was not long before the Corps was expanding into transport and recruiting clerks, accountants, telephonists and storekeepers.

The practice soon spread to the Army Service Corps and to the Women's Royal Air Force (the WRAF) which was formed on the creation of the RAF as a separate service in 1918. Soon, too, women began to fill skilled jobs traditionally thought of as 'men's work', as engineers, fitters, electricians and armourers. Recruits were volunteers and signed on for the duration of the war or for at least one year. Like men, they had to pass selection and medical boards.

With the Women's Royal Naval Service (the WRNS or, more commonly, 'Wrens') moving in the same direction, women had rapidly become an integral part of the armed services. By 1918, some 18,000 had enlisted and about a quarter of them had left for service overseas.

The serving women received official commendations for their work, and Queen Mary herself accepted the position of Commander-in-Chief of the WAAC. Working women – like working men – seldom received such recognition. The munition workers had no commander-in-chief. The 1.5 million working women who had swelled the labour force throughout the war would get no battle honours to emblazon their suffrage banners. But the fruits of victory would be theirs to taste.

On 18 January 1918, the Representation of the People Act, with its clause granting women the vote, came before the House of Lords. To the women anxiously grouped in the precincts, this could be the culmination of a lifetime's struggle. To Lord Curzon, Leader of the House of Lords and President of the Anti-Suffrage League, it was also the end of a road.

107. *Reliable pictures of uniforms can usually be found on photographic postcards, but these girls must have been in fancy dress. Parts of normal military uniform, such as the sailor's collar, were retained, but women usually wore dresses or jackets and skirts; overalls or special garments were also used depending on the job. Civilian clothes – mufti – was worn only at home.*

108.   *These are the correct uniforms for the Wrens: navy blue, of course, and ties and white collars for officers and sailors' collars for the ratings. The WAAC and the Royal Flying Corps (before it became the Royal Air Force) wore khaki. The Navy was quick to recruit women for many shore-based duties including skilled work such as photography, signals and naval intelligence. Serving women could be either 'mobile' and posted anywhere in the UK, or 'immobile' and live at home or in a local hostel. Both branches were subject to the same discipline, and all ranks had two weeks' leave for each year of service.*

Personally, he said, he was still utterly opposed to women's suffrage, but he would not recommend to his peers that they should oppose a majority of some 350 in the House of Commons. He saw no way out but to abstain from voting. Thirteen peers followed his example and 71 voted against, but 134 gave the Bill their support.

A month later it received the Royal Assent. Six million women over the age of thirty who were householders, wives of householders or occupiers of property of an annual value of £5, or who were university graduates, all became entitled to vote.

Millicent Fawcett could sleep soundly in her bed. But then she always had.

6
THE VOTING RIGHT

I N November 1918 – almost simultaneously with the signing of the armistice that ended World War I and only nine months after women over thirty had been granted the vote – the government hurriedly passed an Act giving women the right to stand for election to the House of Commons.

Prime Minister Lloyd George wanted a quick election. The current Parliament had been in existence since 1910; his government was a coalition drawn from all parties, which might have worked well during the crisis of war but could easily come apart in peacetime; and there was much work to be done. A peace treaty had to be negotiated, and President Wilson had produced his Fourteen Points but did not fully understand the European situation. The French, quite naturally, sought military security but also wanted punitive reparations against Germany. Domestically, major changes would be needed. The shift back to a peacetime economy would be as disruptive as going to war, and only recently had economists begun to count the cost. Rationing would have to continue, new industries be developed, and jobs would have to be found for the millions of soldiers returning home, and where were those 'homes fit for heroes' to come from?

Lloyd George knew that he could retain power if more than one party backed his government, so he did a deal with the Conservatives, and between them, they fought the 'coupon election'. At least the soldiers had their vote. Let them use it – and the women too.

The latter were caught unprepared with only a few weeks to organise themselves. Had they been offered votes and candidacies in 1910, hundreds would have come forward to stand for election. Now only seventeen women contested parliamentary seats. Alone among them, Christabel Pankhurst fought as a Lloyd George coalition candidate. The remainder were largely traditional Liberal and Labour with a sprinkling of independents, and included Charlotte Despard, Emmeline Pethick Lawrence and Edith How Martyn.

Only one woman won. Countess Markievicz, the former Constance Gore-Booth and sister of the energetic Eva who with Esther Roper had so enlivened Lancashire, took South Dublin for Sinn Fein. Like her compatriots, she accepted neither the oath of allegiance nor her seat. A wayward spirit she must have been something of an embarrassment to the women's movement, which gained nothing immediately from her success.

109. *Postcards of the general election of 14 December 1918 are very difficult to find. Called in haste only four weeks after the end of the war, postcards were rejoicing in the peace, the return of troops and victory celebrations. This card, though, postally used in 1919, may have been published to mark the occasion. It is only worth reproducing as one of the very first cards to record the fact that women had won the right to vote.*

COUNTESS MARKIEVICZ,
(Who took a prom.nent part in the Rebellion, Stephen's Green Area),
Sentenced to Death;
Sentence commuted to Penal Servitude for Life.

Rosa Luxemburg

LUXEMBURG, ROSA (1871—1919). Founded Polish Socialist Party; always to the fore on the International Left Wing; murdered by reactionaries after the abortive "Spartacist" rising in Berlin, 1919.

Reproduced from the *Plebs* and published by the National Council of Labour Colleges Publishing Society, Ltd., 15 South Hill Park Gardens, London, N.W.3.

110. Above left: *Constance Gore-Booth, who married the Polish Count Markievicz, deserves more than a mention. Although now remembered as the first woman to be elected to Parliament, she first gained prominence for the part she played in the Irish Easter Rising of 1916. The superb gown and aristocratic stance in this photograph hide her revolutionary character. This image may have been taken during her Parisian or theatrical days, and then used by the Sinn Fein propagandists for postcards. They distributed cards of many of their fighters, and the roughly guillotined sides reveal their amateur skills.*

Countess Markievicz bore prison life well, refusing to let hard labour stop her from maintaining her personal life or writing regularly to her sister Eva. She was less concerned with politics than with freedom and substance less than style. In prison, she asked visitors to bring her asparagus and, when reprieved and released in 1917, had no regard for money. Ten years later, she died penniless in a public ward at the age of 51.

111. Above right: *Rosa Luxemburg was another female revolutionary who attracted attention during World War I. A Polish socialist, she attempted to use the collapse of the old order to bring about genuine social and economic changes. In 1919, she was associated with the abortive 'Spartacist,' (i.e. Communist) uprising in Berlin and was murdered while being taken to prison. This card commemorates her more as a socialist than a feminist.*

The first woman to take her seat in the House of Commons as an MP was Nancy Astor, who won a by-election in her husband's old constituency in Plymouth on his elevation to the Lords in 1919. This really was an occasion for celebration. Arthur Balfour and Lloyd George acted as her sponsors and the press fully reported a woman's story that, for once, was not about militancy, marriage, the war or scandal. In 1921, she was joined by Mrs Wintringham following another by-election.

Suddenly MPs found that all legislation had a woman's angle. Conscious of having to win their votes, they sought their advice on every issue. Some MPs had thought that, once women got the vote, they would support a women's political party but this did not happen. The structure of the parties remained unchanged. The women's organisations were themselves unsure how to act; their leadership had concentrated on winning the vote, their members on winning the war.

In the NUWSS, many members felt they should now use the power of the vote to bring about a whole host of desirable changes. To some extent, it was the same argument that the pacifists had used during the war, but there was much wider agreement on the need for improvements in education, health and social services. The purists, however, held true to the

Westminster : Our Lady M.P.'s

112. *The first women MPs received good media coverage. This postcard of Nancy Astor and Mrs Wintringham was published by Pathé Frères Cinema Ltd and would have featured in their news reels. Astor was a Conservative and Wintringham a Liberal, but they worked together in the House on matters affecting women. They had also both won seats formerly held by their husbands – a way of entry to the House not much considered by the suffrage movement.*

concept of acting solely with regard to women's own position, and feared that they would lose independence by becoming involved with other causes. These were not essential differences but, rather, symptoms of the new environment in which women now found themselves. Having directed their attention for so long towards winning the vote, they had given little thought as to how they might use it. Faced with new circumstances, they agreed on a new name – the National Union of Societies for Equal Citizenship – and Millicent Fawcett, her work completed, handed over the presidency to Eleanor Rathbone. Secretary of the Liverpool Society since 1898 and daughter of an MP, she was to become an Independent Member of Parliament for the Combined Universities from 1929 to 1945 and lead a new generation.

They soon had something to get their teeth into. The Sex Disqualification (Removal) Act, passed in 1919, was intended to eliminate barriers preventing women from following many careers. It succeeded immediately in the legal profession – to which it had been primarily directed – and women became magistrates and qualified as lawyers. Other professions acted similarly but the Civil Service was less compliant. Not only had there been signs of uncooperative attitudes among civil servants during the drafting of the Bill, but when it became law, women encountered entrenched opposition against allowing them into the higher grades. It looked as if the government was dragging its feet, and in 1920, questions had to be raised in the House. It was not until 1921 that satisfactory procedures were introduced, but there were still long delays before they were implemented. Looking back, this prevarication can be seen as less significant as a breakthrough by the women's movement than as an example of the near impossibility of legislating against prejudice.

The elections of 1922, 1923 and 1924

The surprising sequence of elections in the early 1920s found women better prepared. Lloyd George was the great loser; his Conservative allies had turned against him, the Liberals split and Labour was now capable of standing on its own feet. Women did well, and postcards showed renewed vitality.

More than forty women contested the three elections and eight of them won seats in 1923 – three Conservatives, three Labour and two Liberals. This number fell to four with the swing against the first-ever Labour government in 1924, but women's ability to contest and win seats had been clearly established.

By now the position of the majority of women was being better understood. A weakness of the Sex Disqualification Act was that it dealt only with the fringes of women's employment. That women could now become barristers or chartered accountants was fine for the handful of those who wanted to do so, but the Act did nothing for women in countless other occupations who faced discrimination every day. The criticism that had been levelled at the movement since Victorian times – that it was the province of a few well-educated, middle-class women – could now be said to have been proved in practical terms.

113. Top: *During the war women had been taught how to apply 'Marcel' waves, originally a male preserve. Although many lost their jobs in the postwar reconstruction, with women earning money more was spent on women's wants and jobs in hairdressing grew. This postcard from 1919 was a 'give away' with a romantic novel, another growing market.*

114. Above: *Women's greatest breakthrough in employment came in clerical and office work, their rapid mastery of the typewriter giving them the edge over men. Files were maintained in vast warehouse-type buildings like the one pictured in this postcard where employment was on a scale comparable with an industrial or manufacturing process.*

A WOMAN CAN NOW HAVE
HER SEAT IN PARLIAMENT!

"You vote as I vote or I'll know
the reason why!"

Do vote for me
Sincerely
Julia Jorrocks
Oxford General Election 1923

115. Above left: *This postcard would have been produced for the 1922 election but, along with others in the set, would no doubt also have been used in 1923 and 1924. They were drawn by Fred Spurgin, a noted comic artist but lacking the sharp insight of some of the pre-war political cartoonists. It is a pity that the arrival in Parliament of women MPs was rated no more highly than a seaside joke.*

116. Above right: *Another typical card of the 1920s and one that might have been used up to the 1935 election. The comic postcard view of women has shifted from suffrage meetings dominated by women to polling stations and the domineering wife.*

117. Left: *Parliamentary candidates often used postcards for publicity. This one, autographed by Julia Jorrocks, Oxford candidate in the 1923 general election, is particularly striking. In 1920, Oxford University had admitted women to full membership with degrees, academic dress and shared control. And here was Julia Jorrocks as a parliamentary candidate with fashionable hat, scarf, jacket and casually drooping cigarette – the very epitome of the 1920s woman. The Edwardian suffragists seem an age away. Jorrocks did not win.*

After the war, a large number of women were unemployed. Most of these were the munitions workers who had to relinquish their jobs to the men returning from the war. The fact that working practices also reverted to pre-war conditions meant that women had to accept the same disadvantages as before. Poorly paid, barred from skilled work and with little opportunity for overtime, they lacked the means of protecting their position. In 1919, Mary MacArthur's National Federation of Women Workers merged with the General and Municipal Workers Union (now the GMBTU) to increase its bargaining power, and other women's trade unions were absorbed into the TUC.

The Civil Service had also laid off large numbers of women. For clerical workers, however, the prospects of finding other jobs were much better. The typewriter, the telephone and the absence of organised resistance from men provided increasing opportunities for women. They quickly established themselves and, having typing skills, became indispensable, but they still earned far less money than men: women office workers were paid a little over £1 a week while men received twice as much.

Domestic employment offered jobs as well – not so much on a living-in basis as had been the pre-war pattern, but none the less involving long and inconvenient working hours and idiosyncratic conditions of employment. These were hardly the circumstances to attract women who had worked in industry, served with the troops and had learned to stand alone.

By 1921, when the postwar upheavals had settled, working women still made up only 29 per cent of the working population, exactly the same proportion as in 1911. To many, it seemed as if they had gained little. To those women MPs of the early 1920s, the situation must have presented a challenge.

Pre-war Factory Acts and those of 1916 and 1920 had dealt with the employment of women in industry but failed to secure the equality which they sought. Wage differences were an obvious example, but difficulties in securing skills, handling only defined work and working specified hours all limited women's opportunities. Worse still, the Factory Acts accentuated women's disabilities by being designed to protect them in same the way that children were protected. They were forbidden, for example, to lift items above a certain weight or to clean moving machinery because of the dangers posed by long hair.

Many of these impediments stemmed from existing working practices and trade union attitudes in looking after male members. Unfortunately women saw no clear solution. On the one hand, the 'equalitarians' would have swept away all differences, while on the other, the 'protectionists' believed that many women needed special conditions of work. Attempts in 1924 to draft a new Factory Bill which could deal with these matters failed and the differences remained unresolved.

Inequalities in other occupations also became apparent as women began to press for recognition in areas where they had previously been excluded. The cautious Civil Service, no doubt still gasping from the concessions which had already been wrung from it, still required women to leave on marriage, and other employers followed their lead. In teaching, where women had been the first to press their claim for equal pay, Lord Burnham's Committee granted them only five sixths of men's salaries, and another precedent had been set.

However, on many issues, the 1920s saw women making valuable progress. The Widows' Pension Act granted them rights similar to the old age pension; the Matrimonial Causes Act made the grounds for divorce the same for women as for men; the Midwives and Maternity Act at last regularised the circumstances for childbirth; and women's rights concerning children were covered by Acts controlling guardianship and adoption.

As to ownership of property, the Law of Property Act gave equality on intestacy to husbands, wives and children, and the Maintenance Acts stipulated the husband's responsibilities to the family. Indeed in this respect, property laws became more onerous to men than to women and the 'equalitarians' – as if to demonstrate their objectivity – set out to rectify them.

By far the greatest achievement in the 1920s occurred in 1928 with the reduction in women's voting age from thirty years to twenty-one.

The 'flapper vote' and the election of 1929

It was Stanley Baldwin who had redeemed his party's pledge to eliminate the anomaly of a higher voting age for women than for men, and it had been backed in the House of Commons by the huge majority of 387 to 10. Baldwin was criticised by some of his colleagues for enfranchising younger women who might let in a Labour government. Although the Labour Party did take office, it did not have an overall majority, and its victory owed more to the collapse of the Liberal Party than to socialist idealism among the 'flappers'.

"Me and my Boy Friend, My Boy Friend and me,
There isn't much difference between us, but he
Wears his Hair and his Skirts a bit longer than me."

5584

CANDIDATES---AND THE FLAPPERS' VOTE!

BIG MAJORITY   ALSO RAN   LEFT AT THE POST

118.   Top: *In the 1920s and 1930s, fashion-conscious people went for Oxford bags and Fair Isle pullovers. This card has no doubts about the relative status of the sexes – the woman is even taller than the man.*

119.   Above: *D. Tempest drew many comic postcards but few with a political flavour. He did not have to look very far to see humour in the 1929 election.*

COPYRIGHT
Miss Margaret Bondfield, M.P.
WALTER SCOTT.
BRADFORD

NATIONAL CONFERENCE OF LABOUR WOMEN
TOWN HALL, BIRMINGHAM

The Chairman

The Secretary

MAY
27th
&
28th,
1925

Photo: Guttenberg, Manchester.
Miss Ellen Wilkinson, M.P.

Dr. Marion Phillips

120. Top: *Margaret Bondfield won her seat at Northampton in 1923 at the age of 50. Leaving school at 13, she had had an exceptional career through the trade union movement and chaired the General Council of the TUC. She got her political education from the Labour Party, and although she worked for women's suffrage, she did not see the suffrage movement doing much for the working class. She was a junior minister in the short-lived Labour government of 1924 and reached the Cabinet as Minister of Labour in 1929 – a first for women on both occasions.*

121. Above: *Ellen Wilkinson, red haired and 'Red' had the rare distinction of winning a seat for Labour in the 1924 election when the Conservatives regained power. Later she became MP for Jarrow and played a leading part in their hunger march. Her career reached a peak as Minister of Education in Clement Atlee's 1945 government, but she died in office in 1947.*

"Now! Where's my Vote?"

THE FLAPPER VOTE IS ALL THE RAGE.
WE'LL SOON BE VOTING AT MY AGE!

122. & **123.**   *Women artists – Mabel Lucie Attwell and Dora Dean – joined in the flappers' fun. Postcards offered women opportunities that they were quick to take. Following in the footsteps of Kate Greenaway and Beatrix Potter, Mabel Lucie Attwell was one who achieved great popular success and her postcards are today sought after by collectors.*

For the women's movement, the election was a great success. No fewer than 69 women contested the election and 14 of them won – an increase from only four in the previous Parliament. Ramsay MacDonald, as head of the Labour government, also appointed the first woman to the Cabinet – Margaret Bondfield as Minister of Labour.

The breakthrough meant more than just dry statistics and the bargaining for the levers of power. It was a moment when, for the first time, women seem to have been accepted as natural equals to men. Whatever else the younger women did, they brought an air of freshness to a stale scene. With their better education, they showed interest in everything, and they helped to stamp an image on the age which is far more remembered today than those fourteen seats in Parliament.

Postcards helped to awake the public to the new phenomenon. No longer were women portrayed as gorgons who terrorised meetings or Amazons battling with police. Nor were they now the butt of all the jokes. Postcards welcomed the voter of the 1920s,

and the election cards displayed a quality and quantity not seen since Edwardian days.

The election also provided instances of comic irony: whether Margaret Bondfield's official papers as a minister should refer to her as 'she' or 'he'; and George Lansbury, also in the Cabinet as Commissioner of Works, cheerfully chatting with George V on the ailments of old age – but the pleasures of the promised land did not last long. A few months after the government had taken office came the Wall Street crash and chaos in the world's financial markets. Bankers, economists and politicians sought in vain for answers; expenditure had to be controlled and budgets balanced. There were calls for national unity, and as economic activity declined, the depression of the 1930s was ushered in.

Working women possibly suffered more than men. Temporary and part-time workers were among the first to lose their jobs, and all the barriers of discrimination were even more difficult to surmount. But in the face of national adversity, the women's case was but one of many to harassed politicians.

124-129. *This series of postcards by that seaside chauvinist Donald McGill marks a major change from pre-war days and sets the scene for the 'flapper election'. It is difficult to imagine any of McGill's women as suffragettes – but all of them know how to vote.*

"When Father says 'Vote' - we all vote!"

"One man - one vote!"

"Where are you going to, my pretty Maid?"
"I'm going a-voting Sir," she said.   Maid?"
"And who shall you vote for, my pretty
"That Duck in plus fours, kind sir" she said.

Mary has a little vote,
    The same as me and you;
But she don't know what Gladstone said
    In Eighteen Sixty-Two!

"No dear, you haven't got a vote
    — you must wait till the next
        Election!"

"Here Reggie, just hold Poogles a
    minute while I go in and save
        the country!"

Throughout the 1930s, Eleanor Rathbone constantly argued in the House of Commons that more assistance should be given to women who have the responsibility of bringing up families. Sometimes, with men unemployed, a working wife became the breadwinner; often it was she and the children who suffered most. Rathbone illustrated her case by referring to some of the Continental countries which had introduced regular family allowances in order to sustain reasonable standards of living. Her voice was heeded, but not without reservations from the women themselves, some of whom feared that such support would simply tie wives and mothers to the household and deny them the freedom of choice for which they had campaigned.

Ellen Wilkinson wanted much more fundamental change and was quite prepared to take dramatic action. She saw a socialist solution, and led a march of the unemployed – from her constituency at Jarrow to London, a distance of almost 300 miles – to back her argument. They marched for a month, a ragged but dogged column showing the country their plight. Sometimes towns welcomed them with a good, hot, sit-down meal; sometimes they provided a tea urn in a field. The marchers spent nights on schoolroom floors, and when it rained, they got soaked and often slept in damp clothes. Ellen Wilkinson was usually at the head of the march, cajoling, encouraging, exhorting them on. When they reached London, she led them between the high buildings and along the wide uncomprehending streets to present their petition to Parliament. The House received her kindly, but as she heard the sympathetic but bland replies from ministers, she must have understood how the pre-war suffragists had felt. But it was not as a suffragist that she spoke. She had led a march of 200 men, as the MP of the men and women of her constituency.

Women and society

The parliamentary tussles of the 1920s and 1930s are one aspect of the women's movement. During those years, women themselves were unsure of the part that Parliament should play now that they had the vote. There had been talk of a 'women's party', and after the electoral victories of 1929, Nancy Astor had actually suggested to all her female colleagues that they might work as a group, but the idea did not find favour. Also, the nature of parliamentary representation had taken a form not envisaged by the suffragists. It might have been natural, or even commendable, opportunism by Nancy Astor and Mrs Wintringham to take advantage of the vacancies in their husbands' seats, but Mrs Philipson had continued the pattern in 1923 and then in 1928 and 1929 Mrs Runciman and Mrs Dalton both won by-elections in succession to their husbands. Could ties between wives and husbands be stronger than those between women?

Baldwin had perhaps put his finger on it. The subjection of women, he had said, would no longer depend on any creation of the law or need to be remedied by legal action; women would have the fullest legal rights and the grounds for the old agitation had gone. With the disappearance of legal disabilities – and most had disappeared although some additional action would still be necessary – it would be for women to decide how they wished to lead their lives.

This sounded much simpler than it was. The role of the family – which was the unwritten debate accompanying Eleanor Rathbone's pleas in Parliament – illustrated the complexity. How many women wanted any change to their roles as wives and mothers? And did they really have any choice? They now appeared to be free from legal constraints whereas the financial responsibility for family dependants still lay entirely with men. This, of course, was regularly cited as one of the grounds for higher pay for men and thus added to the confusion over equal pay. And did women simply want the right to work? Here was a situation which lay at the heart of women's freedom.

Women themselves, without recourse to Parliament or activist committees, unveiled one new solution. In 1918, Marie Stopes published *Married Love* and introduced ideas of family planning and female sexual pleasure. Other women and doctors backed her, and throughout the 1920s and 1930s, women became aware of social and sexual freedoms that earlier generations could not have dreamed of.

Education, as Emily Davies had foreseen, had fostered the growth in women of new ideas and their wide dissemination. It was much more than a technical or academic achievement. For example, women doctors could approach medicine from a female point of view and pass on their knowledge to a female audience. Better educated women, their numbers growing year by year, were able and eager to use such knowledge.

All universities (with the tardy exception of

THE HOUSES OF PARLIAMENT. WESTMINSTER.

"LLOYD GEORGE AMUSED BY MEGAN."

130. Top: *The portrait on this card is of Ida Copeland. She was elected for Stoke on Trent as a Conservative as part of the swing towards the National government after the split in the Labour Party in 1931. Many MPs used this style of card, having simply to fit their photo into the frame.*

131. Above: *Megan Lloyd George followed her father into the House of Commons in 1939 as Liberal MP for Anglesey. Later she joined the Labour Party and won Carmarthen in 1957. With his own career finished by the disillusionment of his Liberal colleagues and the growth of the Labour Party, it must have given Lloyd George great satisfaction to see both his son and his daughter in Parliament.*

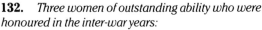

SYBIL THORNDIKE, LL.D., MANCHESTER. (HON.)

LILIAN BAYLIS, M.A., OXON. (HON.)

DAME ETHEL SMYTH, MUS. DOC., DURHAM. (HON.)

REPRODUCED FROM A PORTRAIT BY BERTRAM PARK.

MISS AMY JOHNSON, C.B.E.

132. *Three women of outstanding ability who were honoured in the inter-war years:*
SYBIL THORNDYKE: After taking her degree, she became an acclaimed actress and theatrical manager (and suffragette), and was awarded the DBE in 1931. She died in 1976.
LILIAN BAYLIS: A gifted child violinist, she came to England from South Africa and, in 1898, followed her father as manager of the Royal Victoria Coffee Music Hall, which she transformed into the Old Vic 1912. She also managed Sadler's Wells opera and ballet and was created a Companion of Honour in 1929. In 1937, the year of her death, she attended a suffrage reunion in the Caxton Hall in honour of Charlotte Despard.
DAME ETHEL SMYTH: A musician and composer of international repute, she was the first woman to compose operas in full form. Born in 1858, she had made her reputation by the turn of the century, and was awarded the DBE in 1922. She was an active member of the WSPU, served a prison sentence for window-smashing and was called by Mrs Pankhurst as the only witness at her trial for incitement. She composed the 'March of the Women' and other music for the suffragette bands.

133. *A woman who caught the world's imagination was Amy Johnson. She had been an adventurous child and young woman, running away from home, schools and university. High unemployment meant that the only job open to her was one in a London shop which 'only employed graduates'. She fell in love with aeroplanes and flying and found adventure as well as self-fulfilment. Having raised the money to buy a secondhand Gypsy Moth, she stripped it down and rebuilt it. Only a handful of friends saw her take off from Croydon for Australia on 4 May 1930. When she reached Vienna, the press first took notice of her; by Istanbul, they were writing about her; at Karachi, she received a civic welcome; and when she finally reached Australia, she was world news. The Australians loved it and so did the folks back home. She spent the rest of her life flying, setting records and getting publicity. She died in World War II when, as an airferry pilot in the Air Transport Auxiliary, she crashed near London.*

Her deeds were her memorial. Unfortunately, unlike her great contemporary the American aviator Amelia Earhart, she left no writings from which others might learn.

134. Top: *By the 1930s women were well accustomed to playing a public part in matters which concerned them. Many, like these women in Chelsea, strongly supported efforts through the League of Nations Union to resolve Hitler's territorial claims in Europe by negotiation. In 1934, the Union organised a canvass of over 11 million people, aimed at encouraging disarmament, and embarrassed the National government which had been moving away from collective security.*

135. Above: *Soon after women won the vote, other inequalities – not easily dealt with by legislation – became more apparent. Advertisements such as this one for the Stone's Chop House seemed to make a virtue of discrimination.*

Cambridge) had by now admitted women as full members and secured careers for their students. During the inter-war years, women regularly marked up 'firsts' or new achievements in areas that had previously been closed to them and which their education had now made possible.

With their long and successful experience as teachers, they were ready to take one step more to become university lecturers. Many women who had worked in industry or commerce climbed the career ladder into managerial positions; and with women's long involvement in voluntary and public work, others soon succeeded as local authority officers. The range of achievement was so wide that occupations that resisted women's entry, such as stockbroking and the diplomatic service, soon gained the type of notoriety which had once been accorded to the early feminists themselves. Public opinion had swung in favour of women, and those who achieved outstanding success – such as Mrs Hamilton who was appointed a governor of the BBC – also achieved public recognition. Postcards, too, often offered their plaudits.

Having won such general acceptance, women did not lose their sense of independence. They had their own ideas and priorities. In Parliament, with the major parties haggling over the powers of minority governments or hammering out electoral pacts, a handful of women still made their presence felt. In the 1920s, they ran national campaigns for the protection of children, both in the family and at school, and got legislation on to the statute book. In the 1930s, with depression dulling the domestic scene and Fascism forming thunder clouds abroad, some women spoke out fearlessly. The Duchess of Atholl, who had won Perth & Kinross for the Conservatives in 1923 and had been an Under Secretary of State in Baldwin's 1924 government, was prepared to contest official party policy. She supported the Republicans against the Axis powers in the Spanish Civil War and opposed Chamberlain's policy of appeasement. In 1938, after his fateful meeting with Hitler, she decided to fight a by-election in opposition to the party line. She lost, but history was to prove her right.

As might be expected, this flowering of women's ideas and capabilities was accompanied by new styles in women's writing. For over a century, women writers had been at the forefront of feminism; now they wrote with a new sense of freedom and understanding. In *Testament of Youth* and other books, Vera Brittain described her own experiences in a way that enabled other women to relate them to theirs; Rose Macaulay and Vita Sackville-West explored the appearance and reality of women; and with Virginia Woolf counselling women to keep that 'room of one's own' where their personalities could thrive, the new generation was not short of guides.

Writers and commentators opened up the mysteries of Freud. Psychoanalysis, like Post-Impressionist painting, marks one of the cleanest breaks between the 20th century and the Victorian age. Here was something really new. With psychology playing such an important part in everybody's lives, it would certainly be as important for women as for men. What's more, it was bound to be different, and the search for the female psyche began.

Women now had better grounds for dismissing any charge of inferiority than ever before. By 1939, women had had the vote for just twenty-one years and had used their votes wisely and well; millions of women had jobs and careers; thousands had had excellent education; some of them had achieved outstanding success and some of those had national and international reputations.

Then in September of that year began the war that was to change the lives of everybody in Europe.

7

LYING FALLOW

SPEAKING in 1967 at a conference organised by the Fawcett Society entitled 'Women in a Changing World', Mlle Chaton, who chaired the Committee of Non-Governmental Organisations at UNESCO, wondered what Dame Millicent Fawcett would have thought of the position now achieved by women. Would she be pleased or, with her indomitable fighting spirit, would she write a new book with the title *The Victory Without Results?*

Chaton was well placed to pose such a question. Reviewing women's progress in European countries, she could see that, whereas much had been achieved in Scandinavia, little progress had been made in most other countries since the end of World War II, twenty-two years earlier. In Great Britain, she felt that the most conspicuous failures had been in government (both national and local), the trade unions and the Chambers of Commerce.

Other speakers at the conference, and other writers before and since, dealt with many of the factors which led Mlle Chaton to make her judgement. The evidence that postcards supply confirms her comments even though this is, for different reasons, meagre.

The popularity of postcards had started to decline before World War II. With radio and telephones providing entertainment and communication, the card with a picture on it began to fall from fashion. Publishers sought to cut costs by using cheaper printing techniques, and the quality and variety of postcards gradually gave way to mass-produced scenic views. The war accelerated this process. With troops spread as far afield as North Africa and the Far East, postcards were not the ideal message bearers that they had been in the first war. The armed forces and the Post Office developed new means of communication, and a more literate population wanted more than a square of cardboard on which to write. The trend continued in the postwar period. You sent postcards from holiday spots to wish that friends were there; at home, you watched television. Keeping a postcard album was something that grandma had done – like blacking the kitchen stove.

Of course, postcards were still used, but they had lost the originality of earlier years. Many of them depicted women, but these lacked individuality, as if the whole sex had become some seaside stereotype. A few caught the truth of the moment, of women in a changing society – or women changing as society stood still. There is a temptation to see these few postcards as a reflection of the stagnation in the women's movement to which Mlle Chaton referred, but this would be an overstatement. There are few postcards because they themselves were in decline.

World War II

That women contributed as much to the war effort during World War II as they had during World War I goes without saying. And since it was not said, postcards rarely bothered to record it.

There was a great deal that was left unsaid. Cicely Hamilton, writing on 'The Englishwoman' for the British Council in the first year of the war, had to pick her words with care. The role of the British Council is to tell people in other countries about Britain – its history, culture and way of life. At the outset of a war in which Britain stood alone, the Council needed books and pamphlets to explain the British fight for freedom and democracy. Hamilton deftly summarised the suffragists' struggle and said how the suffragettes' violence and law-breaking so astonished the nation, adding, in parenthesis, that the English were a law-abiding nation. She set out the laws that had been changed in favour of women – but mentioned in passing that legalities still barred Viscountess Rhondda from taking her seat in the House of Lords. 'In theory,' she wrote, women had the same rights as men, but she doubted if women would become judges or ambassadors for another generation – and as for married women losing their jobs, most gave up work on marriage in any case.

W.A.T.S. the use of worrying?

"What do you think about Civil Defence?"

"I believe in it—but if a boy won't take 'no' for an answer then a girl should sock him!"

ALL MY OWN WORK BY GRIMES   With acknowledgments To "THE STAR"

"Can't 'elp about your operations. I've got to do my spring cleaning."

136. Above left: *After their exploits in the First World War women's involvement in World War II was generally taken for granted. As this card shows, women and men stood shoulder to shoulder. 'W.A.T.S.' were the initials of the Women's Auxiliary Territorial Service which had been formed just prior to the war to follow the original WAACS. It was soon referred to simply as the ATS and was later renamed as the Women's Royal Army Corps – the WRAC.*

137. Above right: *Joining the services was seen as the patriotic thing to do – by women as well as men. Recruitment was high at the outset of the war, but by 1941, all young women were conscripted – whatever their views on civil defence.*

138. Left: *RAF operations rooms were the nerve centres of the Battle of Britain. Radar enabled senior officers to organise fighter squadrons against the bombers, and WRAF air traffic controllers replicated the radar information with models on large-scale maps. Official propaganda tended to glamorise their role, but to most women, they were just doing a job like any other.*

Heroic Deeds of the War

MISS MARY CORNISH

The Liner "City of Benares" was crossing the Atlantic to America with 90 little children aboard, evacuees to a land of safety. MISS MARY CORNISH was acting as one of the escort to the children. The Liner was torpedoed. MISS CORNISH took charge of six of the children in a lifeboat, and they were in that open boat for *eight days* before a Flying Boat sighted them 600 miles from land.—Crouched in a corner of the little boat, she told stories to the children, massaged their frozen limbs, and encouraged them to exercise to counteract the bitter cold.—For her inspiring courage, she was honoured with the Medal of the Order of the British Empire (Civil Division).

W533J

139. *During the Second World War, no woman fired the public imagination as had Edith Cavell in World War I, but women's heroism did not go unnoticed. Mary Cornish was escorting evacuee children to the United States when their ship, the* City of Benares, *was torpedoed. She looked after six children in an open boat for eight days until an aircraft spotted them. She told them stories, massaged their limbs and made them exercise to keep out the cold. For this, she received the OBE.*

These point having been discreetly made, Cicely Hamilton could then get down to the job of telling how women had been volunteering for all manner of war work. They were working with men in the new air raid posts of the ARP. In her own London borough, eight first aid centres had been set up, each one with a woman commandant. All over the country, women had enlisted for medical services, fire fighting and the care or evacuation of children. As in World War I, many were going back to the factories and housewives were taking in billeted troops. Women's

Corps, disbanded after 1918, had been re-established by the military and there was no shortage of recruits.

Perhaps because of all that they had done in World War I, women were taken for granted. In fact, in this war they did far more. Immediate mobilisation meant that some served for the whole six years of the war in contrast to the shorter period in the previous conflict. From the autumn of 1940, the blitz over London and other towns and cities brought the war home to the whole population and made women an essential part of overstretched public services. In the following year, women between the ages of twenty and thirty were conscripted into the military services or industry, and by 1943, the age band was widened to take in those between eighteen and fifty years. No other country went so far in systematically mobilising women.

A second generation learned of the traditional prejudices of boyfriends and families towards girls in uniform, and of serving men slowly shifting from being 'anti' to toleration and to final enthusiasm. The large number of women entering the services posed new problems, and led to questions in Parliament about morality, men, and to newspapers running headlines such as 'WILD TALES OF DRINKING AND BAD CONDUCT'. Early in 1942, the government set up a committee under the chairmanship of Violet Markham CH, JP to report on the conditions in the women's services and make recommendations. MPs Thelma Cazalet-Keir and Edith Summerskill along with Mrs Walter Elliot and Mrs J. L. Stocks served on the committee with a phalanx of military top brass. They took evidence from anybody who offered it, toured camps, visited military units, and inspected training schools and hostels. They came up with forty-four recommendations to improve conditions for serving women – and although one of these was the provision of sex education, they found no evidence of immorality.

Women's involvement and integration into the services continued apace. Women officers took command over men, both junior officers and other ranks; women from the ATS jointly staffed with soldiers the 'ack-ack' batteries of the Royal Artillery; and the YMCAs evolved into Young Mixed Christian Associations. As the war drew to a close, women had done all that had been asked of them and more. Their pay had been two thirds of the male equivalent but, unlike their predecessors of the First World War, there was no special reward awaiting them.

The postwar years

If the government and the media had taken women for granted during World War II, it seemed as if women took themselves for granted in the years that followed.

It was only to be expected that after such a war – the second in the lifetimes of many women – there would be a desire for a return to a more settled way of life, and that, having survived the conflict of nations, the comforts of family would be more appreciated. Moreover, many women no doubt felt that they had now gained equality with men. The total conscription of the war had enabled them all to work alongside men, and millions continued to do so afterwards. War-time custom had allowed women to pay their own way on evenings out. After the war, the incomes of those who continued to work gave them a degree

140. *Rationing continued long after the war, and post-war austerity curtailed the purchase of postcards as well as clothes and household goods. Those that did appear showed a return to traditional attitudes. Women were once again seen simply as adornments – the pin-up and the sex symbol created by the cinema of the 1940s.*

WELL GIRLS, WHEN IT COMES TO ECONOMY WE CAN SHOW 'EM SOMETHING.

I won't have you coming into the office looking like a man Miss Potts !

141. *By the 1950s, the rights of all women, single or married, to work in most occupations had been established. Legal rights, however, could not eradicate in-bred prejudice – nor prevent postcards from cashing in on sexual innuendo.*

of independence, and the growing acceptance of birth control reinforced it. For many, these advantages could enhance family life.

To the disappointment of the leaders of the women's movement, very few women seemed to want to use their freedom in public life. The 1945 election had been envisaged as another great step forward: 24 women MPs had been elected, more than double the pre-war number. It was thought that this would lead to more gains, but despite the fact that 126 women candidates stood in 1950, only 21 were elected. The total dropped to 17 a year later, before settling back into the 20s.

Any thought of an ever-increasing women's influence in Parliament had to be deferred. As disheartening as the small number of seats was the fact that most of the MPs and candidates came from women's groups that had cut their political teeth in the years before the war. The thirty-year-olds who had grown up since the vote had been won, and who should have been the future leaders, were not coming forward. There was talk of more co-ordinated action by women, but many thought that votes were lost by accentuating solely women's issues. Women had equality and should use it. Some of the leading MPs, among them Barbara Castle who had entered the house in 1945, wanted the parliamentary careers that men had and to hold the ministerial appointments they held.

Meanwhile the freedom of the female population continued to increase steadily. It was evolution, not revolution — the progress that so many women had perhaps rightly taken for granted. Soon women made up a quarter of all university places; Oxford, and later Cambridge, removed restrictions on the number of women students they would accept; the House of Lords at last agreed that women would be let in, and the Civil Service withdrew its injunction that married women must be kept out.

It was married women who experienced the most changes. Ten years after the war, about half of the 7 million working women were married and using their income to help support the family home. They married younger and more of them chose to do so. The days of having to choose exclusively between marriage or a career were safely consigned to the past. Public attitudes towards divorce and family planning hurried to keep up, and both Church and State accorded them recognition if not benediction and bounty.

The younger married woman also set the pace for commerce and industry. The extraordinary expansion of women's magazines (*Woman* alone had a circulation of over 3 million) was but the peak of a pyramid of products, advertised through their pages, aimed at female consumers. An endless range of goods for the home — from the kitchen to the spare bedroom — gave the 'houseproud' woman all that she might need and whatever else the market researchers might induce her to buy. Later feminists came to reject this 'consumerism', and it was not something that Mlle Chaton would have seen as success. But after the austerity of the postwar years, it offered countless women and their families a standard of living that they had not previously enjoyed.

Equal pay

Mlle Chaton also failed to mention equal pay, an issue that stretched back to Victorian times and one of the most obvious inequalities between women and men. The initially weak position of women as piece-rate workers, the struggle of the pit-brow women, women's own willingness to accept any pay for the chance of a job, their lack of trade union bargaining power and the exigences of two world wars, all seemed to cement inequality into working life.

Equal pay had actually been the issue that had brought about the one defeat of Churchill's war-time government. In the debate on the 1944 Education Bill, Thelma Cazalet-Keir had introduced an amendment that teachers' salaries should have no differentiation between men and women solely on the grounds of sex. Seconded by Peter Thorneycroft — later a

142. *After losing her seat in the House of Commons, Thelma Cazalet-Keir chaired the Equal Pay Campaign from 1947. A Conservative, she had always had close links with other political parties and public figures, as the speakers at this meeting bear witness. It would have been held in the early 1950s between the award of her CBE in 1952 and the success of her efforts in achieving equal pay for teachers and civil servants in 1955.*

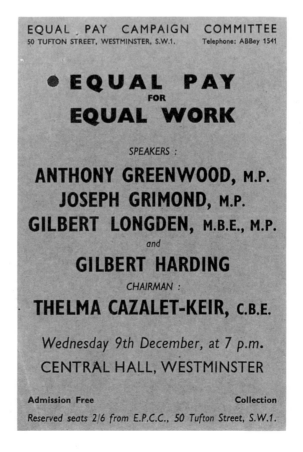

EQUAL PAY CAMPAIGN COMMITTEE
50 TUFTON STREET, WESTMINSTER, S.W.1.   Telephone: ABBey 1541

● **EQUAL PAY**
FOR
EQUAL WORK

SPEAKERS :

ANTHONY GREENWOOD, M.P.
JOSEPH GRIMOND, M.P.
GILBERT LONGDEN, M.B.E., M.P.
and
GILBERT HARDING
CHAIRMAN :
THELMA CAZALET-KEIR, C.B.E.

Wednesday 9th December, at 7 p.m.
CENTRAL HALL, WESTMINSTER

Admission Free   Collection
Reserved seats 2/6 from E.P.C.C., 50 Tufton Street, S.W.1.

Conservative Chancellor of the Exchequer and, as Lord Thorneycroft, Chairman of his Party – the amendment was won by a single vote – 117 to 116. Churchill must have remembered those suffragette days and his Manchester by-election, for with only two weeks to go before the D-Day landings, he made the issue of equal pay into a vote of confidence and the amendment was duly deleted. Nevertheless, he set up a Royal Commission to consider equal pay, and appointed Thelma Cazalet-Keir as Parliamentary Secretary to the Ministry of Education in his caretaker government of 1945.

The Royal Commission produced little that was new and completely ruled out any extension of equal pay to industrial workers. However, teachers and civil servants were more strongly organised and, with Thelma Cazalet-Keir now out of Parliament and chairing the Equal Pay Campaign Committee, they mounted an old-style campaign of meetings, demonstrations and petitions. The growing shortage of teachers helped their cause, and in 1955, the government accepted their demands but spread the increase of women's salaries over a seven-year period.

Much sterner opposition came from industrial workers, and they were partly helped by the ambivalence of the Trades Union Congress. Nevertheless in 1963, women succeeded in getting a 'Charter for Women' backed by the TUC, which called for real equality, not just in pay but in all aspects of women's working life – promotion, training and welfare. A majority of unions officially supported the approach, but in the workplace, the changes could seldom be brought about, and in the heartland of manufacturing industry, where apprenticeships, craft demarcations and skill differentials governed all bargaining, the unions remained opposed. It took a strike by the women at Fords in 1968 to force the issue. They won and received such backing that, in the same year, women were able to compel the TUC to accept that industrial action could be used as a tactic to gain equal pay.

The time was right for action by the Labour government. The prospect of claims by women confusing an already complex and inefficient system

"YOU UNION MEN ARE ALL THE SAME — STICKING OUT UNTIL YOU GET WHAT YOU WANT!"

143. *Postcards deteriorated in quality throughout the 1960s. The crudity of the colours and of captions, such as the one on this card, are obvious. Its only redeeming feature is that it reflects the stance of the industrial trade unions against equal pay for women.*

of industrial relations had to be avoided. In 1970, Barbara Castle took the opportunity of introducing the government's Equal Pay Act and it received support from all sides of the House. Progress towards implementation was slow but assisted by Mlle Defrenne's case, under Article 119 of the Treaty of Rome, against Sabena Airlines for equal treatment with male cabin staff. None the less it became apparent that lower pay was due as much to women's exclusion from skilled work and training as it was from different pay levels. They lacked opportunities as well as equal pay.

8
REVIVAL

T HE Equal Pay Act of 1970 was far from being the last word in an argument that had begun 100 years earlier; nor does it specifically mark the change in the women's movement which was to become so apparent in the 1970s and 1980s. Women's attitudes had, in fact, been changing for a decade.

Much of this was the result of influences from overseas. The writings of Simone de Beauvoir and Anaïs Nin had become increasingly important since the war, and in 1963, Betty Friedan's *The Feminine Mystique* was published simultaneously in the US and the UK. The United States provided much of the stimulus, the civil rights movement there making women conscious of the limitations in their own liberty. Their efforts resulted in such ear-catching phrases as 'The Comfortable Concentration Camp' (Betty Friedan) and 'burning the bra' (allegedly from

144. & **145.** *Attempts to repeal the 1967 Abortion Act by limiting its application united women liberationists. These postcards were sponsored as propaganda material by the National Abortion Campaign, a feminist group set up in 1975 to protect women's rights to legal methods of abortion. The NAC canvassed support from the public and from influential organisations and succeeded in winning the backing of the TUC. It also worked closely with the women MPs who successfully blocked various Private Members' Bills put forward by James White (1976), William Benyon (1977) and John Corrie (1979). The campaign's strength lay in the argument that women should have the right to choose.*

146. *This postcard by Jill Posener showing a Lambeth street in 1978 neatly puts the plight of women in the context of a rundown city centre. The women's liberation movement had been arguing that the National Health Service should supply free contraceptives.*

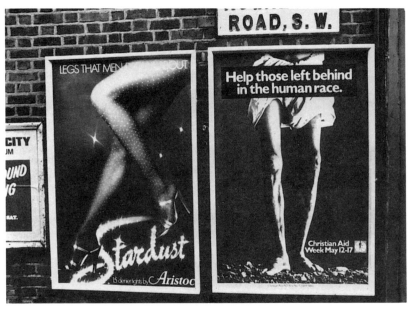

147. *Mike Wells uses the same technique in a picture taken in Fulham in 1980. The sexist consumerism of modern advertising which appalled so many women liberationists is put to shame by the desperate circumstances of people elsewhere.*

148. *Daubing slogans on walls and billboards was popular with the new feminists – and if you could spoil sexist image-forming advertisements at the same time, so much the better. Jill Posener also succeeds in underlining women's growing awareness of a fundamental antagonism between women and men.*

149. Above left: *Cath Tate had a much simpler message. Women should recognise their own strength and use it by joining the Labour Party. This postcard was part of a campaign to strengthen the women's organisation within that party.*

150. Above right: *Many women were concerned with more than just freedom expressed in political terms. For some, feminism also meant being able to express their own personalities free from the romantic mould in which men had cast them.*

151. Left: *This is one of the few postcards produced by commercial publishers which noticed the liberationists. Published by Bamforth & Co of Holmfirth who had sold cards since 1902, this one had moved a long way from their famous romantic and sentimental song cards of the Edwardian period.*

152. *Here Jill Posener is again emphasising women's right to freedom. If advertising aimed at heterosexuals is acceptable, why shouldn't women with an alternative sexual identity be free to go their own way?*

153. *Sue Sanders catches an equally eloquent picture during Gay Pride week in London in 1979.*

an incident at the Miss America contest of 1968). These travelled easily across the Atlantic but did not fully express women's frustration at having to fill roles that others had assigned to them, whether these be the suffocating involvement with the family or a male judgement on the attributes of female beauty. A similar phrase, and further impetus to the movement, came later with Germaine Greer's *The Female Eunuch* (1970).

Words such as these found a ready audience among British women brought up in the postwar consumer society who faced male prejudice when they went out to work. Free from the exhaustion of war and more widely educated both in schools and universities, they were ready to reconsider their position in society. They relished the de-bunking of Freud; they read of female sexuality; and the pill did

for the 1960s and 1970s what other forms of birth control had done for the 1920s and 1930s.

The first National Women's Liberation Conference was held in 1970. Those involved simply wanted to explore where women stood by exchanging views with each other and that over 500 came was ample proof of the underlying support. They did not see themselves as descendants of Victorian suffragists or Edwardian militants. Nevertheless, they were soon political activists. Having set up a National Coordinating Committee and study groups on special subjects, demonstrations were organised against that year's Miss World competition at the Albert Hall as well as marches for equal pay, education and support for contraception and abortion. With the last two items, they were breaking new ground and trying to bridge the gap between motherhood and a career.

Parliamentary progress

There was no doubt in politicians' minds that women's issues now needed special attention, and the 1970s saw a marked increase in women's involvement in parliamentary affairs. The average number of women candidates at the six elections between 1951 and 1970 had been 87. In the two elections of 1974, the numbers rose to 143 and 161, and in 1979, reached 206. Unfortunately the numbers elected remained much the same and in 1979 actually declined to only 19. But women were clearly ready and willing to participate. It could no longer be argued that the new liberation movement simply comprised extremists. There was now growing evidence of a groundswell of dissatisfaction among women throughout the country.

The political parties responded by devoting large parts of their manifestos to women's affairs. The Labour Party, which was closest to the women liberationists, went as far as to develop a special charter for women and a detailed list of their needs: equality of treatment in social security; allowances, nursery schools and day care for children; divorce and separation rights; and umbrella legislation on sex discrimination. Apart from less emphasis on working mothers, the Conservatives seemed to differ mainly on the choice of words: child credit for mothers; pensions for married women; widows' benefits; and an 'Equal Opportunities Commission' to deal with discrimination. The Liberals stood solid on their long history of support for women's rights and doubtless referred to their large number of female candidates.

Such a unique political consensus for assistance to women, and the impending International Women's Year in 1975, brought results in the Sex Discrimination Act of that year. Joyce Butler, a Labour MP, had started the ball rolling in 1967 with a Private Member's Bill which had failed. Then in 1972 Willie Hamilton, another in a line of socialist sympathisers, and Baroness Seear introduced similar Bills in the Commons and the Lords. Hamilton's ran into trouble despite Caxton Hall meetings and a march on Downing Street recalling suffragist days; but Baroness Seear's Anti-Discrimination No. 2 Bill went forward to a select committee. In the spirit of the old NUWSS, it took evidence from a broad range of opinion and eventually won over all doubters. Edward Heath's Conservative government, however, then announced that it would introduce legislation of its own, and when these proposals were overtaken by the general election, the task fell to the new Labour government. Although their Act, which became law on 29 December 1975, did not have the support of all of the women MPs, some of whom felt it would be difficult to enforce, it firmly established the principle of equal rights.

Women's Year had left its mark. The government had brought in the Social Security (Pensions) Act which made special provision for women's rights in retirement, and the Employment Protection Act safeguarding them during maternity. In opposition, the Conservatives had elected Margaret Thatcher as leader. It is ironic that this seemed to cause more consternation to some women than to most men.

An issue which united the women MPs and showed just how effective they could be was the possibility of Parliament making changes to the Abortion Act of 1967, which had originally been introduced by the Liberal David Steel as a Private Member's Bill. The women MPs were now drawn into the fray by the attempts of other MPs to limit its application. As public debate grew, the women came to realise that they were representing a far broader constituency of women, one which went beyond normal party allegiances. Acting as a group, they saw, too, that male MPs, while willing to support them, did not rate the issue as having any great importance and they were left to organise procedural opposition and lobbying themselves. Working with organisations outside the House such as the National Abortion Campaign, they backed the normal methods of dissent: marches, meetings and petitions. They fought three Private Members' Bills – two under a Labour government and one under a Conservative – and beat all three of them. The strength of their case was not directly related to abortion as such, but to the argument that women should have the right to decide what happens to their own bodies. That men would not concede this simply reinforced their determination.

It was just the right subject for the women's movement to start using postcards again.

The renaissance of postcards

The dull uniformity which had clothed postcards through the postwar decades provided the background for the rediscovery of the brilliance and originality of their Victorian and Edwardian predecessors. Old albums which had lain unopened for fifty years and collections of cards which had slept in chests of drawers were suddenly seen by new collectors. They marvelled at their quality, at the rich chromolithographic printing and the sure line of the artists, and were amazed by the variety and range. They wrote articles about them, published books and formed clubs. Then in 1970 the Victoria & Albert Museum's Centenary Exhibition provided the seal of approval.

Much of their appeal stemmed from nostalgia. As collectors unearthed the roots, so the enthusiasm for postcards increased. The reawakened interest in these cards was entirely different from the revival in the women's movement. Women were breaking new ground and seeking something fresh. To postcard enthusiasts, the rediscovery of the original cards was an end in itself. Women sought to create something new; old postcards recreated the past.

The interest in postcards did not, therefore, immediately influence present-day publishers, who remained sceptical of the market potential for higher-quality short-run cards. However, towards the end of the 1970s small individual publishers such as private art galleries, photographers or organisations seeking publicity began to issue them. Some had a political or social angle to promote, and among these were those with a feminist viewpoint.

These cards illustrate aspects of the Liberation movement. Most were not political campaigning cards as such. They did not tell the recipient to vote for somebody or do something, but they integrated the feminist argument into pictures which carried their own message. In this, they differed considerably from the Edwardian suffragist postcards which had quite literal styles to get their message across. In those days, the commercial publishers had made the running and the women's cause arrived late on the scene; now it was the women themselves who were setting the pace. Moreover, it was often women who produced the cards as photographers, artists and publishers, and they have continued to do so.

The Thatcher phenomenon

Postcards have some affinity with newspapers: they both print what the public likes to see and what it likes to read. Postcards did not celebrate the moment when women finally won the vote nor did newspapers give the story much coverage. For both, there were more pressing subjects, and after all, it was a foregone conclusion. The momentous election of Britain's first woman Prime Minister in 1979 seems to have been greeted by postcard publishers with similar disdain, although, this time, newspapers, aware that readers look to them for more detailed information, gave her success a little more space than they might have a man's.

The media is also more moved by bad news than good. Politicians suffer from this. It is their failures which are reported and their controversies which are discussed. Early postcards of Mrs Thatcher treated her similarly.

The Falklands war changed all that. Suddenly a wave of patriotic jingoism, the like of which had not been seen since the 'khaki' election of 1900, swept the country. For many, it was simply 'my country right or wrong', and such chauvinism – in the original

meaning of the word – turned Margaret Thatcher into a national heroine.

Others saw the reverse argument – that unnecessary force was being used and that normal channels of international conciliation had been ignored. The debate sparked party rivalry, and became entwined with the anti-nuclear campaign in which so many women played a prominent part and which they illustrated so brilliantly with postcards.

Postcards had now regained their popularity. Scores of bright original designs replaced the faded viewcards on newsagents' racks. With public relations becoming as important as the product, advertisers sent them through the post, hotels gave them to patrons for free and restaurateurs presented them with the bill. Political propaganda cards continued to flourish. They did not necessarily sell through normal retail outlets, but you could find them in specialist shops, on market stalls and at meetings. Leading politicians once again became a subject for satire. Margaret Thatcher naturally featured in many. As the best-known politician of the 1980s, she could not fail to draw attention both in the UK and overseas.

154. *Another view of the police force, and featuring the new woman Prime Minister. The National Council for Civil Liberties which sponsored this card, was arguing in 1980 that Margaret Thatcher and her Home Secretary William Whitelaw were undermining the freedoms of association, speech and assembly.*

155. *A woman Prime Minister and the blandishments of advertising have not done much to help the ordinary woman with children to feed and clothe.*

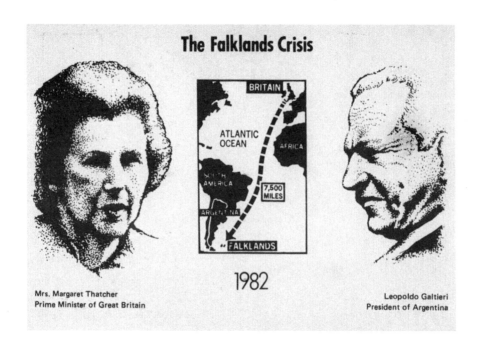

156. & **157.** *The Falklands war gave Margaret Thatcher a major role to play on the world stage and made her a subject for TV satire at home. From being the first woman Prime Minister, she emerged as a national leader who could arouse personal responses – from the very positive to the very negative – in ordinary people in the street.*
Both of these postcards contributed to the revival of the popular theme of commemorating major events, and several publishers produced cards relating to the war. A number were critical of the use of force and continued to be used as anti-government propaganda.

158. & **159.**   *Two of the many postcards of Margaret Thatcher, showing the range of feeling that she has been able to inspire.*

As the years went by, she received the ultimate accolade: commercial publishers themselves began to issue cards of her, and tourists sent them home to Peoria or Dandenong. Whatever else may come to be seen as her achievements either as a woman or as a politician, one measure of her success is not in doubt: she has inspired more postcards than any prime minister since Lloyd George.

Continuing themes

This galaxy of contemporary postcards makes us wonder at the distance the women's movement has travelled over the last 200 years. The cards reveal the depth and strength of women's activities which have grown from those early anguished voices, and allow us to glimpse those ideas and issues which have made feminism the influential force it is today. Like books – in which women have consistently excelled and faithfully chronicled their own development – postcards provide a contemporary commentary of their time.

The political element looms large. Since the Victorian suffragists forced the issue and the suffragettes burned it on our national consciousness, women's rights have been fully acknowledged, but the struggle has moved from the vote itself and beyond the limitations of legislation. Women's legal rights, where so much has been achieved, cannot automatically be translated into changes in everyday life. The plight of the mill girls and the pit-brow women may well have been ameliorated, but contemporary women still encounter barriers to careers and the dual burden of holding down jobs while bringing up families. Similarly the politics of war and peace is not something that can be written into the statute book. The Greenham Common Women are the latest in a line which stretches back to women's involvement in the Peace League of the 1930s and the pacifism of the Labour Party prior to World War I. It is a lineage which might have surprised the Victorian feminists and one with which the first woman Prime Minister has very little sympathy.

160. Top: *Women were closely involved with anti-nuclear protests in the early 1980s. This demonstrator at a Hyde Park rally in 1981 had ideas and allegiances way beyond those of conventional politics.*

161. Above: *This banner, so reminiscent of those used by the suffrage societies, is a copy of the original specially made for the British Council exhibition 'A Woman's Place' held at the Festival Hall in 1984.*

162-164. *It was at the US Air Force base at Greenham Common that the women protestors gained the greatest publicity. The spirit of the women can be seen in these three postcards from a series issued by Acme Cards.*

165. Top: *Both pictorial and literal effect are used in this card by Ed Barber. It was taken at the US base at Upper Heyford where 1,000 people demonstrated in support of the peace camp there.*

166. Above: *Margaret Thatcher and US President Ronald Reagan were often featured on postcards but seldom more effectively than in this photomontage by Cath Tate.*

167. *The rising high unemployment of the 1980s was one of the penalties of the Conservative policy of applying market forces. As on previous occasions, women often suffered more than men but Mrs Thatcher remained adamant. Another Cath Tate photomontage points to a bitter historical precedent.*

168. *Cecil Parkinson fell foul of traditional British moral attitudes towards affairs between married men and unmarried women. This card of the* Private Eye *cover of 31 October 1983 suggested that Margaret Thatcher forced his resignation from the government. However, she welcomed him back to the Cabinet in 1987.*

169. *Cath Tate draws a comparison between increased expenditure by the government on defence in 1985/6 and the reduction in support for hospitals and health care – in particular, the impending closure of this women's hospital.*

170-173. *By the 1980s, political equality was far from being the major concern of many women.*

Nevertheless it is a subject on which women's voices are being heard.

Political action has been most effective on matters directly related to women. Josephine Butler's ghost must have been urging the women on when they successfully fought off the amendments to the Abortion Act. Their cause was the same as hers when she won the repeal of the Contagious Diseases Acts;

and it was the same cause that brought about the revision of the laws of matrimony and childbirth; and which led Teresa Billington to defy the magistrate and his 'man-made laws'. That women should have the right to participate in decisions affecting their own lives is an undeniable political freedom, and one that still unites the movement.

But freedom consists of much more than political rights, and freedom can be expressed in many forms. Contemporary women are still emulating the record breakers of the 1920s and 1930s with ever more 'firsts' and new achievements. We have seen them as High Court judges; as directors and chairpersons of public companies; and as astronauts when, along with men, they have put Puck's girdle roundabout the earth.

After World War II, when the world returned to normality, the longest distance that it was thought proper for women to run in competitive athletics was 400 metres. Gradually the numbers of female athletes grew and the permitted distances lengthened until, now, they run the marathon. When the performances of men and women are compared and the rate of women's improvement is taken into account, it seems possible that a woman will eventually beat a man in the marathon, that ancient test of stamina and endurance.

To a woman facing the combined difficulties of motherhood and career, examples such as these can give her little more than psychological encouragement. That alone could be of value. As more and more women use the opportunities that freedom provides, they move closer towards the ideal status of women of which Mary Wollstonecraft wrote. Their achievements and efforts so far are a vindication in themselves.

Appendix 1
SUMMARY OF KEY DATES

Historical Survey

The Post Office first authorised the use of postcards on 1 October 1870. These though were for cards carrying messages, not pictures; but following the lead in other European countries, postcards bearing pictures soon started to appear. These were usually produced in very small numbers, perhaps by advertisers or individuals, and not encouraged by the Post Office which insisted that one side of the card should be used solely for the address. The practice continued to grow however, and in the 1890s, a few commercial publishers produced postcards with a picture and a small space for a message on one side, with the other side simply having the address and stamp. These are now known as postcards with 'undivided backs'.

It is hardly surprising that among this very limited number of early cards there appear to be no pictures relating to the women's movement. Publishers were thinking only of a popular market and the movement itself was going through a period of quiescence.

Continental countries were again showing a lead by using postcards for political purposes. The Dreyfus affair in France prompted a spate of cards ridiculing the government, and Dreyfus's supporters used cards for lobbying and propaganda. Postcards also began to commemorate special events such as state visits, and when Continental cartoonists started to show sympathy for the Boers in the war with Britain, a number of British publishers responded with some fine patriotic cards.

Queen Victoria's death on 22 January 1901 and the accession of Edward II provided a further stimulus to publishers, and when the Post Office finally authorised the 'divided back' (the address and message on the same side), many of them were ready with full-scale pictures.

This is the beginning of what has become known as the Golden Age of postcards. Countless subjects and varieties were published for more than a decade and many were of very high quality. The political and current affairs themes soon established themselves with the great Tariff Reform debate and the 1906 election.

This was the time when the women's movement first featured, with cards depicting the leading personalities and the 'new women' leaving their husbands to do the washing up. It was now but a short step to the suffrage meetings and the full scale political campaign which came to a climax as the Golden Age reached its peak.

The nature of postcards changed during World War II. Millions of them were still used, but they became more functional rather than being a form of entertainment. The quality declined too – apart from the delicate silk cards that the soldiers sent home from France – due in part to the introduction of cheaper mass-production printing techniques. Nevertheless they left an exceptional record of the war itself. With women taking on roles previously denied them, the postcards give us immediate proof of their achievements.

For both the women's movement and postcards, the inter-war years were a period of consolidation. It was a much more significant period for women than it was for postcards. For the first time, opportunities lay open to them, and their success in taking advantage of these opportunities quelled the last of their detractors. Postcards, now in their maturity as an established form of communication but slowly losing the gaiety and inventiveness of their youth, none the less paid their respects to flourishing feminism.

World War II and the years that followed it transformed everyday life but relegated both the women's movement and postcards to recent history; relics of a bygone age; a time of tranquillity when you could set the clock by the postman's delivery, and a woman's place was seen as being in the home. There was little that they seemed able to add to the welfare state and the days when everybody had '. . . never had it so good'.

Their histories, totally unrelated, had fortuitously followed the same pattern. Suddenly, and again without any direct connection, they both again came to prominence in the late 1960s. Interest in postcards was born of nostalgia; the women's movement found rebirth in a new generation. Separately, in their own fields, they have continued to grow. Postcard publishers once again attract our attention with original designs, and feminist views pervade the media. Once again their two paths have crossed.

The chart set out opposite summarizes the similarities in their development and may help collectors to identify and place their cards.

A CHRONOLOGY OF THE WOMEN'S MOVEMENT AND POSTCARDS

Women's Movement		Postcards
	1790	
Mary Wollstonecraft's *A Vindication of the Rights of Woman*.	**1792**	
	1800	
	1810	
	1820	
William Thompson's 'Appeal of one half of the human race . . .'	**1825**	
	1830	
Mary Smith's petition presented to House of Commons by 'Orator' Hunt.	**1832**	
	1840	
	1850	
Barbara Leigh-Smith forms first feminist group.	**1855**	
	1860	
John Stuart Mill presents women's petition for Franchise to the House of Commons.		
Lydia Becker forms the Manchester Women's Suffrage Committee.		
Richard Pankhurst appears before the High Court for women's right of inclusion in the parliamentary register.	**1868**	
John Stuart Mill publishes *The Subjection of Women*.	**1869**	Austria introduces plain postcards.
	1870	Great Britain follows Austria's lead. Non-pictoral postcards used by women's suffrage groups etc.
	1880	
Repeal of Contagious Diseases Acts.	**1886**	
	1890	
	1894	Post office permits postcards with pictures and undivided backs. Court Cards (squarer) used.
Women's Suffrage Bill reaches 2nd reading.	**1897**	
National Union of Suffrage Societies formed.		
	1899	Postcards of Boer War (Continental & British).
	1900	
	1902	Post Office allows picture postcards to have message and address on the same side. Postcards of the 'New Woman', portraits and some comic cards.
Mrs Pankhurst forms Women's Social and Political Union.	**1903**	
Origins of militancy – House of Commons precincts: May – Free Trade Hall Manchester: October	**1905**	
	1906	Many postcards of general election. Little mention of women.
Leading members of WSPU sent to prison for demonstrating.		
Mrs Despard leaves WSPU to form Women's Freedom League.	**1907**	Wide range of postcards of suffrage campaign produced by: – Commerical publishers;
Suffragist demonstrations of June 13th & 21st.	**1908**	– Women's suffrage societies and other organisations;
Arrest of Mrs Pankhurst, Christabel Pankhurst & Mrs Drummond. Bow Street Trial.		– Independent photographers.

Women's Movement		**Postcards**
Miss Wallace-Dunlop begins first hunger strike. Forcible feeding begins.	**1909**	Wide range of postcards of suffrage campaign produced by:
Lady Constance Lytton as 'Jane Warton' is forcibly fed.	**1910**	– Commerical publishers;
Conciliation Committe and truce. Women in 'Coronation Procession' for George V.	**1911**	– Women's suffrage societies and other organisations;
Conciliation fails – WSPU campaign of violence.		– Independent photographers.
Government's own Reform Bill fails; escalation of violence. 'Cat and Mouse Act'.	**1913**	
Outbreak of WW1. Suffrage societies back government.	**1914**	
Registration scheme for national service includes women.	**1915**	Censorship introduced.
Women become munition workers and take up many other jobs.		During WW1, postcards become more 'patriotic' than 'political', nevertheless many printed and
Government sets up an all-party conference to review franchise.	**1916**	photographic cards recorded women's wartime activities.
Women enter armed forces.	**1917**	
Representation of the Peoples Act grants the vote to women aged 30 and over.	**1918**	Postcard postage rate doubled to 1d.
At general election, Countess Markiewicz becomes first woman to be elected but does not take her seat.		End of postcards' Golden Age.
Nancy Astor wins by-election to become first woman MP.	**1919**	
Sex Disqualification (Removal) Act.		After WW1 interest in postcards began to decline.
	1920	Although the enfranchisement of women in 1918
Eight women elected MPs.	**1923**	was virtually ignored there was growing coverage
Legislation on women's and children's rights.		of womens affairs in the early 1920s rising to a
Voting age for women lowered to 21.	**1928**	peak with the 1929 'flapper' election.
Fourteen women elected MPs.	**1929**	Few cards by women's organisations.
Margaret Bondfield first woman in Cabinet.		
	1930	
Outbreak of WW2; full conscription.	**1939**	
	1940	
Markham Committee reviews women in armed services.	**1942**	In spite of some specialised wartime cards, postcards declined in quality. The habit of
	1950	collecting postcards withered.
Equal pay won for teachers and civil servants.	**1955**	
	1960	
	1961	Formation of the Postcard Club of Great Britain.
TUC backs 'Charter for Women'.	**1963**	
Equal Pay Act.	**1970**	Centenary Exhibition by the Victoria and Albert
First National Women's Liberation Conference.		Museum.
International Women's Year.	**1975**	IPM Catalogue first published.
Sex Discrimination Act.		
Attempt to repeal Abortion Act defeated.	**1976**	First British International Postcard Exhibition.
Attempt to repeal Abortion Act defeated.	**1977**	
	1978	*Picture Postcard Monthly* first published. Independent producers publishing more contemporary postcards.
Attempt to repeal Abortion Act defeated.	**1979**	
Margaret Thatcher becomes Prime Minister.		
	1980	
Women's anti-nuclear campaigns.		Other specialist and commerical publishers begin producing new style postcards.

Appendix 2
DETAILS OF ILLUSTRATIONS

The Individual Items

1. Postcard by an unnamed publisher. Postally used from Hull *c.*1906 but precise date indecipherable.

2. Artist Dudley Buxton. Published by J. Beagles & Co. Ltd.

3. Artist F. Macleod. Published by Henry Garner of the Living Picture Postcard Co. Leicester. Although this company produced many coloured comic cards most were unsigned. The company ceased to trade in 1909 placing this card in the early part of the women's campaign.

4. Published in G. H. Martyn & Sons Series; a sepia print from a photograph.

5. & 6. The Scots artist Martin Anderson, who used the pseudonym 'Cynicus', was an established caricaturist and satirist by 1890. He produced 'hand painted' pictures like these for framing and sale through shops. His technique seemed to be to colour by hand his printed outline. He was commissioned to design postcards in 1898 but returned to Scotland to set up, in 1902, the Cynicus Publishing Co. Ltd., through which he successfully published many series of postcards.

7. W. T. Stead's 'Portraits and Autographs' was published in 1890. The pictures are photo engravings and the names and addresses of the photographers themselves were also given for the benefit of people wishing to collect the photographs themselves.

8. A photographic print by the London Stereoscopic Co. The company produced portrait postcards of politicians for use during the 1906 election.

9. Published by Raphael Tuck and Sons. 'Oilette' type No. 9498, 'The Suffragette' series. Postally used in 1908 – a fairly prompt reaction to the militant campaign.

10. Published by E. Mack, King Henry's Road, Hampstead, London. Artist unknown. Eric Mack came from the Bristol firm of William F. Mack which had been in business as printers and booksellers since 1857 and was, therefore, likely to be well aware of the cartoons and politics of the late Victorian times.

11. Published by Wildt and Kray from series 775.

12. Published by Raphael Tuck and Sons, an 'Oilette' type No. 9202 from Series II 'Cycling and Motoring Jokes from Punch'. The coloured postcard is based on the black and white drawing by the famous 'Punch' artist Bernard Partridge.

13. & 14. As for No. 7.

15. Published by Woolstone Bros, London, under their trade name 'The Milton Postcard'. This is styled a 'Fac-Simile' Series No. 105. Like many early coloured postcards it was printed in Germany at the company's own factory in Saxony.

16. Published by W. Boughton & Sons Ltd. of Thetford, Norfolk; the Britannia Series.

17. Published by Davidson Bros, London and New York; Real Photographic Series No. 4265.

18. Photographic card published by William R. Readhead, Stationer, Flamborough.

19. Real photographic postcard; photographer and publisher unknown.

20. Real photographic postcard; photographer and publisher unknown.

21. Real photographic postcard; photographer and publisher unknown.

22. Published by Millar & Lang, Art Publishers, Glasgow and London in their National Series trade mark. They produced a number of comic cards relating to the Insurance Act.

23. Publisher unknown but printed from a negative by Blake, Stationer, Longton.

24. Artist George A. Bamber. Published by The Corona Publishing Co. Blackpool (Regal Series) 1167.

25. From a series of the early Labour Party MPs published from photographs by Elliott & Fry.

26 & 27. Both of these postcards are from designs of The Cynicus Publishing Co. Ltd., Tayport, Fife, numbers 10035 & 10036. However number 10036 – the Unionist variation – has been used as an advertising card by John Thridgold & Co., Fine Art Publishers of Sidney Street, Commerical Road, London E. The company describes it as a:

'New Style done by the Aerograph Air Brush. Something bright and cheerful. All Good Comics. HUNDREDS OF DESIGNS. Nothing Vulgar.'

and sells samples at 3/- a gross or 18/6 a 1,000.'

The cards do not bear Cynicus's signature but could not be closer to Martin Anderson's style and show how his technique had changed from the 'hand painted' style shown in illustrations 5 and 6.

28. Artist Walter Crane – his rebus in the palette at the foot of the picture shows that he drew the original in 1888. Postcard reproductions of his work, such as this, were used by Socialist Societies but this one is not attributed to any publisher. However the message on the back begins 'Dear Comrade' and it was postally used in 1907.

29. No named publisher but clearly a 'Clarion' postcard. Another message beginning 'Dear Comrade'.

30. Published by John Walker & Co. Ltd., Warwick Lane, London E.C. This company also produced a well-known series of free trade cartoon postcards by Harry Furniss.

31.   Artist G. F. Christie. Published by William Lyon of Glasgow in their 'Premier' Series, No. 2105.

32.   This postcard was published by the WSPU whose name and address – 4, Clements Inn W.C. – is clearly shown. It is from a photograph by Martin Jacolette, South Kensington.

33.   As with number 32, this postcard gives no information other than that shown on the front.

34.   No publisher named and possibly produced by the Labour Party or by supporters of Keir Hardie from a photograph by G. C. Beresford.

35.   As for number 25.

36.   Artist Donald McGill. Publisher unnamed. McGill is perhaps the best known of all postcard artists and designed his first card in 1904. This one is, therefore, amongst his earliest.

37.   Published by Shamrock & Co of Paternoster Row, London. The owner of the company was Felix McGlennon who, given the choice of name and a number of Irish songs amongst his postcards, may well have been Irish. Perhaps he had a fellow feeling with oppressed groups.

38-43.   Artist Arthur Moreland. Published by G. W. Faulkner & Co. Ltd., London, E.C. Series No. 777. Moreland was a leading political cartoonist and did several postcard series for Faulkner.

44 & 45.   Both of these cards were published by Millar and Lang Ltd. in their National Series – numbers 635 & 641. No named artist.

46 &47.   As with numbers 32 & 33, these cards must have been published by the organisation named on the fronts – The Women's Freedom League.

48.   Published by Valentine & Sons Ltd., Dundee. This 'living picture' type of postcard was used by a number of publishers, particularly J. Bamforth & Co. Ltd.

49.   Artist MATT. Printed and published by E. Hulton & Co. Ltd., Manchester, in a booklet issued in 1908 reproducing cartoons of the North West Manchester Election.

50.   Artist's name unclear – D. M. Coates. Published by the Artist's Suffrage League, 259 Kings Road, Chelsea.

51.   Published by the Women's Tax Resistance League, 10 Talbot House, St Martin's Lane, London WC.

52.   Artist Isobel Pocock. Published by the Suffrage Atelier.

53.   From a photo by Ian Campbell. Published by GOMER, number 148. Available from W.F.L.O.E, A. & P., Glangors, Ynyslas, Borth, Dyfed, and from the Fawcett Library, London.

54.   Half-tone photographic print. Published by Sandle Bros, Empire House, Paternoster Row, London, EC. Anthony Byatt in his 'Picture Postcards and their Publishers' states that this card and others similar to it, were published by Sandle Bros on behalf of the NWSPU.

55.   No publisher named.

56.   Privately produced postcard.

57.   Privately produced postcard.

58.   Privately produced postcard.

59.   See No. 32. Photo by Lafayette, Glasgow. This card

was postally used on 8 February 1910 – less than a fortnight after Lady Lytton's release from prison. The message on it reads: 'The pc and return was a joyfull surprise. You may like this martyr, I can't say I feel her one. Did not hear her speak after all, she was ill but hope to later. Liked Mrs P. should prefer Christabel I fancy. May you feel inclinced but *not* militant. And yet stick up for this right and left! Queer me! Will write soon. Fondest love.'

60.   Printed from a photo by Elliott & Fry. No publisher named.

61.   Published by Valentine & Sons Ltd.

62.   Published by the WSPU. The artist's name is surprising and poorly positioned; 'A Patriot' appears under the picture of the Lord.

63.   Published by the Women's Freedom League, 1 Robert Street, Adelphi, WC. No artist named. The back of this card is very informative; it bears the rubber stamp of the Literature Department of the WFL and a hand-written list of 'New Literature Next Week':

In the Workhouse. Play and Preface by Mrs Nevinson. 6d.

Josephine Butler: Cameo Biography. By Mrs Marion Holmes. 2d.

Women's Suffrage and the Health of the Nation. By Dr Haden Guest. 1d.

64.   Photographic postcard. Neither publisher nor photographer named.

65.   From the weekly newspaper of the NUWSS, Parliament Chambers, Great Smith Street, Westminster, London SW. and printed by Percy Brothers Ltd for the Proprietors, The Common Cause Publishing Co. Ltd., 64 Deansgate Arcade, Manchester.

66-72.   Published by Birn Brothers Ltd., 67-70 Bunhill Row, London EC. These cards are taken from two sets numbered E19 and E23. The Birn brothers had started business in the 1880s as importers of quality stationery and fancy goods. Their postcards too were of high quality and, like those illustrated, were usually printed in Germany.

73.   Artists' initials, C.H. and D.M. No publisher named.

74.   A USA postcard requiring a one cent stamp. Walter Wellman had copyright in 1909 and presumably published it – No. 4012.

75.   Printed and published by J. Salmon Ltd., Sevenoaks, Kent.

76.   Published by Valentine & Sons Ltd.

77.   Published by The Photochrome Co. Ltd., London and Tunbridge Wells. From their Celesque Series.

78.   Published by Alfred Stiebel & Co., London EC. From the ALPHA Series No. 299B.

79.   Neither publisher nor artist named.

80.   Published by the London Branch of the Church Socialist League from a photo by H. Harrison.

81.   Photographic postcard by W. J. Willmett, Pier Photographer, Pelham Crescent, Hastings.

82.   Printed and published by The North British Rubber Co. Ltd., Castle Mills, Edinburgh. Makers of famous golf balls.

83.   Photographic postcard by F. Kehrhann, Bexley

Heath, Sussex. From the collection of the Fawcett Library.

84. Printed and published by The Woodland Card Co. Ltd., London EC. Series No. 105.

85. Photographic postcard. Published by Molyneux's Library, William Street, Woolwich. Photographer unnamed.

86. Photographic postcard. Publisher and photographer unknown.

87. Artist Donald McGill. Published by Inter-Art Co., (The International Art Co.), Florence House, Barnes, London SW. "COMIQUE" Series No. 2034.

88. Printed photographic montage. Published by C. & A. G. Lewis, Sherwood Street, Nottingham, in their Colonial Series.

89. Photographic postcard with imprint of E. F. Baldwin, Bath & Cheltenham, in bottom right-hand corner but no indication of exact locality.

90. From a popular series of women at work but no indication of artist or publisher.

91. Published by Millar and Lang Ltd., National Series No. 1228. Artist unnamed.

92. Artist Fred Spurgin. Published by the Art and Humour Publishing Co. Ltd., 27 Chancery Lane, London WC, in their WOMEN WAR WORKERS Series, No. 141. This company was in fact set up early in the war, possibly to fill the gap left by fewer cards being available from overseas.

93. Photographic postcard. Publisher and photographer unknown.

94. Photographic postcard. Published and photographed by F. W. Foulsham, Specialist in Outdoor Photography, 63 Wokingham Road, Reading, Berks.

95. Artist unknown. Published by The Corona Publishing Co., Blackpool. Regal Series 2064.

96. Artist Arthur Butcher. Published by the Inter-Art Co., 'ARTISTIQUE' Series No. 1318.

97. Published by Birn Bros Ltd., London. Series No. W.M. The war forced Birn Bros to switch manufacture to England but with the badge embossed and gilded they maintained their high quality; (see cards Nos. 66-72).

98. No indication of artist or publisher – similar to No. 90.

99. Artist W. Barribal. Published by MACA in the series 'The World's Modern Masters' No. 56. This publisher appears to be Italian and the postcard bears the British 'Passed by Censor' stamp No. 1008.

100. Photographed and published by Elliot & Fry, London.

101. Photographer unknown but the imprint of The Queen Alexandra Military Hospital Extension appears on the back.

102. Printed and published by Laureys, 17 rue d'Enghien, Paris.

103. Artist T. Corbella. Published by the Inter-Art Co as a set. On the back of the card is printed in English, French, Dutch and Italian: '"Kultar" threatens Miss Cavell nursing a wounded enemy.'

104. Published by A. Noyer, Paris.

105. Artist Reg Maurice. Published by The Regent Publishing Co. Ltd., London NW. No. 3257.

106. Printed and published by The Times Press, Bombay.

107. Photographer not known. Presumably from a studio portrait.

108. Photographic postcard; E. F. Driver, Bramford Lane, Ipswich.

109. No indication of artist or publisher.

110. Printed and published by the Powell Press, 22 Parliament Street, Dublin.

111. Reproduced from the 'Plebs' and published by the National Council of Labour Colleges Publishing Society, Ltd., 15 South Hill Park, London NW3.

112. Published by Pathé Frères Cinema Ltd.

113. Published by 'Forget-Me-Not' Novels as a giveaway advertising card. It has the date 19 April 1919 which presumably coincided with the issue of another of their publications.

114. Photographic postcard. Publisher and photographer unknown.

115. Artist Fred Spurgin. Published by Art and Humour Publishing Co. Ltd., Chancery Lane, London WC., in their 'ELECTION' Series No. 1138.

116. Artist unknown. Published by the Inter-Art Co in their 'COMIQUE' Series, No. 6706.

117. Photographic postcard by Hills & Saunders, Oxford.

118. Artist unknown. Published by the Inter-Art Co in their 'COMIQUE' Series No. 5584.

119. Artist D Tempest. Published by Bamforth & Co. Ltd., in their 'COMIC' Series No. 2810.

120. Photographic postcard published by Walter Scott, Bradford.

121. Publisher not named but presumably the Labour Party or the Labour Women. The picture of Ellen Wilkinson is from a photo by Guttenberg, Manchester.

122. Artist Mabel Lucie Attwell. Published by The Carlton Publishing Co., London EC. Series No. 591.

123. Artist Dora Dean. Published by K – C. 'Kiddie' Series No. 1056.

124-129. Artist Donald McGill. Published by Woolstone Bros., London. The company commenced business in 1902 publishing most of their postcards under the trade mark 'Milton'. These cards are also marked 'Renowned' with numbers between 2455 to 2466 – a likely set of 12.

130. Although a standard card used by many MPs, this one has no publishers name. Ida Copeland has autographed it on the back.

131. Published by the Photochrome Co. Ltd., but no photographer named.

132. This reproduction from a portrait by Bertram Park may well have been published by himself as no one else is named.

133. Publishers "Tit Bits" used this card for advertising. No doubt it was given away with their magazine.

134. Photographic postcard. This card, slightly out of focus, resembles Edwardian photographic cards of local events recorded by studio or amateur photographers. Neither the photographer nor the publisher is named.

135. Artist 'Sallon'. Published by Stone's Chop House as an advertising card. On the back are printed quotations from the *Sporting Times* and Charles Dickens recommending the restaurant.

136.   Artist unidentified. Published by XL "CHEERFUL" Series, London EC. No. 18.

137.   Artist M.A. As for No. 136. No. 11.

138.   Artist Grimes. Published by Raphael Tuck & Sons Ltd. From a lengthy but unnumbered series by the regular cartoonist of *The Star.*

139.   Published by the Overseas League, St James's, London, SW1, to send with cigarettes and tobacco to serving men. Money for these was contributed by school children and this postcard enabled the troops to scribble a note of thanks.

140.   No indication of artist or publisher.

141.   Artist 'T.K.'. Published by Sunshine Comic. No. 5601.

142.   Leaflet published by the Equal Pay Campaign Committee, 50 Tufton Street, Westminster SW1.

143.   Artist Pedro. Published by Sunny Pedro Series. No. 110.

144.   Artist Liz Mackie. Published by Leeds Postcards, 13 Claremont Grove, Leeds 3. The back carries a slogan 'Defend a woman's right to choose!'.

145.   Artist Catriona Sinclair. Published by Leeds Postcards. The back gives brief details of the abortion campaign.

146.   Photo by Jill Posener. Published by Deviant Productions. Unit 160, 27 Clerkenwell Close, London EC1.

147.   Photo by Mike Wells. Printed by Penshurst Press Ltd.

148.   Photo by Jill Posener. Published by Deviant Productions.

149.   Photomontage by Cath Tate. Published by the C.L.P.D. Women's Action Committee, 39 Calverdale Road, London SW4 9LY.

150.   Published by Dodo Design (Mfrs) Ltd., 1 Warwick Park, Tunbridge Wells, Kent. 'Dodo's Doomsday Cards. One of a set of shock-horror-probe postcards taking a sideways glance at topics of universal concern to mankind and other nonsense.' Ref: 233 275300.

151.   Artist Chas. Published by Bamforth & Co. Ltd., in their 'COMIC' Series no. 644.

152.   Photo by Jill Posener. Published by Deviant Productions.

153.   Photo by Sue Sanders. Published by Deviant Productions.

154.   Artist John Minnion. Published by Leeds Postcards. Sponsored by the National Council for Civil Liberties, 186 Kings Cross Road, London WC1X 9DE. The back gives details of the organisation and its objectives.

155.   Photograph from 'Real Freedom: Women's Liberation and Socialism' by Kate Marshall. Junius Publications BCM JP Ltd. London, WC1N 3XX.

156.   Published, designed and printed by KQP Ltd., Mansfield, Notts. A 'KING CARD'. A limited edition of 2,000 cards. Design 201.

157.   Designed and published by FAGA and printed by Southern Printers, Shirley, Southampton. Postcard No. 352. The back of the card gives the key to the localities

numbered on the map. It also lists other cards in the series. FAGA was one of the leaders of the postwar revival of postcards having begun publishing them in the 1960s.

158.   Artist Syd Brak. Published by Athena International, London. No. 9375. 'Maggie'.

159.   Artist Oscar da Costa. Published by Athena International. No. 9251. 'Margaret Thatcher'.

160.   Photographed and published by Ed Barber. Printed by Expressions Printers Ltd., London N7.

161.   Photograph by K Morris. Published by GOMER, W.F.L.O.E., A. & P. Glangors, Ynyslas, Borth, Dyfed, SY24 5JU.

162, 163 & 164.   Published by ACME CARDS, London. From a series, numbers: NK15 − Singing peace songs outside USAF Greenham Common after "embracing the base", 12 December 1982. Photo by Mike Goldwater/ Network; RP4 − Blockade of Gate 6 at USAF Greenham Common, 14 December 1982, as workers arrive by bus to build Cruise Missile silos. Photo by Raissa Page; RP1 − 1 January 1983: women dance at dawn on a Cruise Missile silo site in USAF Greenham Common. Photo by Raissa Page.

165.   Photograph by Ed Barber. Published by Leeds Postcards. Originally published by Leeds Postcards as part of the 'Common Cause' 1983.

166.   Photomontage by Cath Tate. 'A Special Relationship'. Printed by Blackrose Press (TU), 30 Clerkenwell Close, London, EC1.

167.   Photomontage by Cath Tate. Printed by Blackrose Press.

168.   Taken from the Private Eye Bumper Book of Covers. Published by Eagle Editions. Plain back card.

169.   Photomontage by Cath Tate. Printed by Blackrose Press. 'Who is going to missile your hospital?' The back gives details of Tory expenditure on defence, hospitals and community health services.

170.   Artist Jacky Fleming. Published by Leeds Postcards. 'Jobs for the Girls'. Originally published for Woman Alive an event organised jointly by Marxism Today and the Communist Party.

171.   Photograph by Chrissie Thirlaway. Published by Cath Tate, P.O. Box 647, London SW2 4JX. 'Lying on cars'. Plain back card.

172.   Artist Viv Quillin. Published by Cath Tate Cards. No. CT46. 'Monica'.

173.   Artist Annie Lawson, P.O. Box 910, London SE14 6DD.

Types, Rarity and Prices

The above list makes immediately apparent the variety and range of postcards. They can be photographic, printed or photo-printed; black and white, toned or coloured; the quality can vary enormously within any category and the skill of an artist can provide individuality; most are produced commercially, others for publicity and propaganda, and some for privte use.

These distinctions are particularly pronounced in the period to WW1 as interest in postcards flourished with the   opportunities   offered   by   technological developments in photography and printing. Thereafter cheaper mass-production methods tended to standardise the quality so that the period following WW1 became characterised by large runs of more predictable cards. Interestingly the revival of postcards has come when technology is once again providing new opportunities in colour photography and printing.

More and more collectors are coming to appreciate these distinctions. This is particularly true of photographic cards for which collectors and dealers now make a very clear distinction between the individual photographs by independent photographers and those produced in larger quantities by new processes such as rotary photographic printing. The former often reflect the immediacy of the moment (for example Nos. 19 and 81) while the latter often appear to be more professionally prepared and more carefully posed (No. 17). For many years these two types continued side by side and sometimes they come happily together (No. 37).

Equally significant was the way in which photography became integrated into traditional printing. At the turn of the century, photographic images were being etched on sensitised plates to provide prints. The quality of some of these was high and continued to improve (No. 54). Printing itself was going through a revolution with the introduction of three-colour printing stimulating many new processes (Nos. 26 and 27). While this enabled postcard publishers to offer a very wide range of cards it also meant that there was considerable variation in the quality (contrast Birn Bros, Nos. 66-72 with the unknown publisher of No. 109).

The subject matter of a postcard is of course of prime interest to a collector but the quality of the picture can enhance its impact and the technique of its production can decisively influence its rarity. In recent years, both the quality and the rarity of early 'real photographic' cards has come to be fully appreciated and some of these relate to the processions and campaigns of the militant period of the women's movement.

Photographers who produced such cards in the London area include:

A. Barratt, 8 Salisbury Court, Fleet Street.
Christina Broome, Fulham, SW.
Muriel Darton, 45 Stapleton Hall Road, N.
Scotts Studios, Regents Park, NW.
H. Seargeant, 159 Ladbrooke Grove, W.

Photographers who took the chance of recording by-elections, meetings, campaigns and similar events in their own locality include:

E. W. Bradden, Guildford.
Harold H. Camburn, Tunbridge Wells.
S. Cribb, Portsmouth.
George Davis, Oxford.
A. E. Graham, Redcar.
S. G. Griffiths, Haverfordwest.
A. Henderson, Cambridge.
H. Jackson & Son, Liverpool.
Herbert Morris, Newton Abbot.
Ross, Whitby.
W. Strickland, Liverpool.
Winifred Turner, Chichester.
E. Anthony Tyler, Stratford on Avon.
J. White & Son, Littlehampton.
W. White, Wolverhampton.

Photographic postcards have been seen from many other localities but without attribution.

In the totality of postcards up to the revival in the 1970s, those relating to the women's movement are scarce. Any immediately command a premium price. Factors such as the subject matter, the demand in relation to the numbers available, the quality and the rarity, determine the range of prices at which cards are sold. Many of the commonest – some comic cards or women at work – are priced at about £3 but some can rise to £5 or more with better cartoons and propaganda material issued by the suffrage movement reaching £10 to £15. Similar prices are asked for portraits of leaders and well-known personalities. Campaigning pictures reach the highest levels of up to £25 or more when collectors of women's cards compete with local historians for the rarer photographic items.

For cards issued in the last twenty years, prices are much more reasonable and many still sell at original retail levels of between 15p and 40p. Some, however, are especially collected and Liz Mackie's Abortion Campaign card (No. 144), for example, sells at considerable premium.

Within this overall framework individiual cards must be judged separately; features such as the work of a particular artist or a photographer, or even the message on the back, may need to be taken into account. The women's movement – especially the suffrage campaign – is a specialist subject and any collector would benefit from learning more of it.

Appendix 3
NOTES ON THE DEVELOPMENT OF POSTCARD COLLECTING

Postcards have always been collected. Even the publishers of some of the early cards with undivided backs produced them with the collector in mind. Raphael Tuck's 'Empire Series' issued at the turn of the century is an example of high quality cards following a theme so that they could be displayed as a collection. Many cards were produced in sets – usually six – with the same purpose in mind.

Postcard users and collectors responded eagerly. The messages on the backs of Edwardian cards often refer to the sender's collection, suggest arrangements for exchanging cards, or ask for special ones to be sent. Soon they were being put into albums. Magazines for collectors appeared, clubs were formed and competitions organised.

It was this enthusiasm, from collectors and publishers alike, which gave the Edwardian period its special quality. Many of the collections were a mixture of cards reflecting the whims of the collector and the wanderings of the correspondents; others concentrated on a particular subject and postcards of the women's movement often fall into this category as sympathisers or active workers followed the campaign.

The hobby of collecting continued during World War I as postcard albums formed a link with absent families and friends, but after the war, with so many changes and diversions such as radios and cars, postcards were gradually forgotten. Some collectors persevered but the cards were usually records of holidays or family portraits. This waning of enthusiasm undoubtedly played its part in the postcard's decline.

The discovery of these original collections and the sense of nostalgia they evoked sparked the revived interest of the 1960s and rekindled the desire to collect. Many of the albums were broken up as collectors sought out the cards they wanted most: pictures of their home town; vintage motor cars; *fin de siècle* frou-frou – or suffragettes.

Responding to collectors' desires, a network of dealers sprang up like ice cream salesmen on a sunny seaside promenade. They came from antique markets, second-hand bookshops and the philatelic world. Soon they were followed by auctioneers and organisers of fairs until, with competitions, clubs and magazines, the hobby had recreated its Edwardian past.

Today, there are postcard fairs almost every weekend, auctions are held regularly, and it is estimated that there are more than 300 dealers. For someone wishing to find out more about the hobby, the following information will be of use:

Catalogues and Magazines

IPM Catalogue of Picture Postcards. Published by IPM Publications, P.O. Box 190, Lewes, Sussex, BNZ 1HF.

RF Picture Postcard Catalogue. Published by RF Postcards, 17 Hilary Crescent, Rayleigh, Essex.

Collect Modern Postcards. Published by Reflections of a Bygone Age, 15 Debdale Lane, Keyworth, Nottingham, NG12 5HT.

Picture Postcard Monthly. Published by Reflections of a Bygone Age, 15 Debdale Lane, Keyworth, Nottingham, NG12 5HT.

British Postcard Collectors Magazine. Published by R. Griffiths, 47 Long Arrotts, Hemel Hempstead, Herts, HP1 3EX.

Some Dealers in Postcards and Accessories

Daphne Abel, 11 Nevill Road, Hove, Sussex.

Bluebird Arts (J. A. Foster), 1 Mount Street, Cromer, Norfolk.

Branch Two (Robert Jeeves), 36 Queen's Road, Brighton, Sussex.

CAMRABUKS (Colin Derbyshire), 6 Cambridge Road, Ellesmere Port, South Wirrall.

DUCAL (Jack and Thelma Duke), 228A Shirley Road, Southampton, Hampshire.

E. W. Postcards (Eric and Wyn Wooley), 14 Beach Road, Bilston, West Midlands.

Edwardian Postcards (Freda Gittos), Nastend House, Nr Stonehouse, Gloucestershire.

J. A. L. Franks Ltd., 7 New Oxford Street, London WC1.

Michael Goldsmith, 16 Heron Road, St Margarets, Twickenham.

Goulborn Collection (Karlyn Goulborn), 44 Highfield Park, Rhyl, Clwyd.

J. H. D. Smith, International Postcard Market, P.O. Box 190, Lewes, Sussex.

Kirkgate Postcards, Duncan Chambers, 9 Duncan Street, Leeds.

Leeds Postcards, P.O. Box 84, Leeds, LS1 4HU.

Peter Lincoln Postcards, 75 Nags Head Hill, St George, Bristol.

Brian Lund Postcards, 15 Debdale Lane, Keyworth, Nottingham.

Liz McKernan, 356 Ditchling Road, Brighton, Sussex.

MEMORIES (Clive Smith), 18 Bell Lane, Hendon London NW4.

Micklegate Collectors Centre (Tony Dyche), 63 Micklegate, York.

PANDORA (Bill Musgrove), New Antiques Centre, 27 New Street, Plymouth, Devon.

Mick Portsmouth, 6 Cecil Court, Charing Cross Road, London WC2.

R. F. Postcards, 17 Hilary Crescent, Rayleigh, Essex.

RAYMAR Collectors Centre (Ray Shapland), Barum House, 1 Bear Street, Barnstaple, N. Devon.

S & D Postcard Co. (Sita Winstone), Great Western Antique Centre, Bartlett Street, Bath.

SHELRON (Ron Grosvenor and Nova Saunders), Yealm House, 9 Brackley Road, Towcester, Northants.

Jill Smith, 7 Darlington Gardens, Shirley, Southampton.

Stenlake and McCourt (Richard Stenlake), 1 Overdale Street, Langside, Glasgow.

Lynn Tait Gallery, 85A Chalkwell Esplanade, Westcliff-on-Sea, Essex.

TAMARISK BOOKS (Anne Taylor), 89 High Street, Hastings, East Sussex.

Some Auctioneers

Barum Auctions, Barum House, 1 Bear Street, Barnstaple, Devon.

Christies South Kensington, 85 Old Brompton Road, London SW7.

Elm Hill Stamps and Coins, 27 Elm Hill, Norwich, Norfolk.

Garnet Langton, Burlington Arcade, Bournemouth, Dorset.

Phillips West Two, 10 Salem Road, London W2.

Shelron, Yealm House, 9 Brackley Road, Towcester, Northants.

Sotheby's Chester, Booth Mansion, 28 Watergate Street, Chester.

Specialised Postcard Auctions (K. Lawson), Corinium Galleries, 25 Gloucester Street, Cirencester, Gloucestershire.

Fairs

Postcard fairs have become the most popular way of buying and selling postcards. The annual 'BIPEX' organised by the Postcard Traders Association is now well established. It is held every September in Kensington Town Hall with more than sixty leading dealers present for four days. The PTA has now begun to organise similar functions outside London.

Other postcard fairs – some with even more dealers attending – take place regularly throughout the country. These range from large monthly fairs in London and Manchester to regular programmes in other locations and periodic events in many towns.

Information about these fairs will usually be found in the local press. Advance information can be obtained from fair organisers, of whom there are now about fifty, including the following:

C. S. Fairs, Hyanis House, Bromsgrove Road, Romsley, Halesowen, West Midlands.

Ron Emmott Promotions, Fourways, Church Hill, Westend, Southampton.

IPM Promotions, P.O. Box 190, Lewes, Sussex.

Leeds Postcard Fairs, 37 Kirkdale Crescent, Leeds.

Piccadilly Plaza Exhibitions Ltd., York Street, Manchester.

R. F. Postcards, Specialist Postcard Fairs, 17 Hilary Crescent, Rayleigh, Essex.

Clubs

Recent years have seen a rapid growth in the formation of postcard clubs. As more and more collectors have found pleasure in meeting each other, they have grown up usually on a local basis but sometimes in relation to an interest in a particular subject. Over fifty are now in existence and almost all of them hold regular meetings.

Membership of a club is one of the best ways of learning about the hobby, since it provides contact with other collectors and local dealers both of whom can usually offer advice and guidance. Details of clubs – location, secretaries, events etc – are given in the Picture Postcard Annual published by Reflections of a Bygone Age.

SELECT
BIBLIOGRAPHY

The Women's Movement

Balfour, B. *Letters of Constance Lytton*. William Heinemann Ltd, 1925.

Blease, W. Lyon *The Emancipation of English Women*. David Nutt, 1913.

Blythe, R. *The Age of Illusion*. Hamish Hamiliton, 1963.

Coote, A. & Campbell, B. *Sweet Freedom*. Basil Blackwell, 1982.

Eisenstein, H. *Contemporary Feminist Thought*. Unwin Paperbacks, 1984.

Freiden, B. *The Feminine Mystique*. Victor Gollancz Ltd, 1963.

—————— *The Second Stage*. Michael Joseph.

Fulford, R. *Votes for Women*. Faber and Faber, 1957.

Hamilton, C. *The English Woman. British Life & Thought*. The British Council, 1940.

Harris, S. *Women at Work*. Batsford Academic & Educ. Ltd. 1981.

Holtby, W. *Women*. The Bodley Head, 1934.

Hopkins, H. *The New Look*. Secker and Warburg, 1964.

Mitchell, J. & Oakley, A. *The Rights and Wrongs of Women*. Pelican Books, 1976.

Nicholson, J. *Kiss the Girls Good-Bye*. Hutchinson & Co.

Peel, C. S. *How We Lived Then*. John Lane, The Bodley Head Ltd, 1929.

Rosen, A. *Rise Up Women!* Routledge & Kegan Paul, 1974.

Rover, C. *Women's Suffrage & Party Politics in Britain 1886–1914*. Routledge & Kegan Paul, 1967.

—————— *Love, Morals and the Feminists*. Routledge & Kegan Paul, 1970.

Showalter, E. *A Literature of Their Own*. Virago, 1978.

Stead, W. T. *Portraits & Autographs*. The Review of Reviews, 1890.

Strachey, R. *The Cause*. G Bell & Sons Ltd, 1928.

Tickner, L. *The Spectacle of Women*. Chatto and Windus, 1987.

Vallence, E. *Women in the House*. The Athlone Press, 1979.

Woolf, V. *Three Guineas, A Room of One's Own*. The Hogarth Press, 1938.

Postcards

Atkinson, D. *Mrs Broom's Suffragette Photographs*. Dirk Nishen Publishing, 1989.

Byatt, A. *Picture Postcards and Their Publishers*. Golden Age Postcard Books, 1978.

Davies, P. *Collect Modern Postcards*. Reflections of a Bygone Age, 1987.

Duval, W. & Monahan, V. *Collecting Postcards*. Blandford Press, 1978.

Holt, T. & V. *Picture Postcards of The Golden Age*. MacGibbon & Key, 1971.

Lund, B. & M. *Picture Postcard Monthly*. (March 1983; February 1985; October 1986; September 1988; & others). Reflections of a Bygone Age.

Smith, J. H. D. *IPM Catalogue of Picture Postcards & Year Book 1989*. IPM Publications.

Staff, F. *The Picture Postcard & Its Origins*. Lutterworth, 1966.

INDEX